WAR DIARY

Also by Yevgenia Belorusets

Lucky Breaks
Modern Animal

WAR DIARY

Yevgenia Belorusets

Translated from the German by Greg Nissan

New Directions / ISOLARII

The author would like to thank Christoph Scheuermann, Alla Zamanska, Mark Belorusets, Mariana Golovko-Danchenko, Sebastian Unger, and Kyrylo Tkachenko for their conversation and presence during these days, and thanks also to Alina Kleitman, Daria Kuzmych, Nikita Kadan, Eugene Ostashevsky, Sebastian Clark, Daniel Medin, and Christina Belous.

Manufactured in the United States of America
First published as a New Directions Paperbook Original (NDP1553) in 2023
Book design by Dan Visel

Library of Congress Cataloging-in-Publication Data
Names: Belorusets, Yevgenia, author. | Nissan, Greg, translator.
Title: War diary / Yevgenia Belorusets ; translated from the German by Greg Nissan.
Description: New York : New Directions Publishing ; ISOLARII, [2023] |
"First published as a New Directions Paperbook (NDP) in 2023."
Identifiers: LCCN 2022050539 | ISBN 9780811234801 (paperback) |
ISBN 9780811234818 (ebook)
Subjects: LCSH: Belorusets, Yevgenia—Diaries. | Ukraine—History—Russian Invasion, 2022—Personal narratives. | Kyïv (Ukraine)—History—21st century. |
Journalists—Ukraine—Kyïv—Biography. | Kyïv (Ukraine)—Biography.
Classification: LCC DK508.852 .B45 2023 | DDC 947.7086—dc23/eng/20221021
LC record available at https://lccn.loc.gov/2022050539

War Diary is a copublication by New Directions Publishing and ISOLARII.

New Directions Books are published for James Laughlin
by New Directions Publishing Corporation
80 Eighth Avenue, New York 10011
ndbooks.com

ISOLARII is a media company devoted to providing orientation in a deteriorating world
isolarii.com

CONTENTS

Why is there fire on this path?

Preface
March 16, 2014–July 16, 2022

When the war first started in 2014, it wasn't clear that it was actually war. It dressed itself in the form of a revolution, a protest mounted by the newly invented *people of the Donbas*. It sold itself as an allegedly *peaceful* and *civil* annexation of Crimea. The peacefulness as well as the civility of this process were supposed to point to something other than war. But to this day, that something has no name of its own.

In the spring of 2014 while I was living in Berlin, I listened to the news reports of the Donbas events from various sources. It felt like I was being lied to from almost every side. Crimea had already been annexed; Russian tanks were on the move in eastern Ukraine. Here in Germany, a blind eye was turned to the tanks and the heavy artillery. At that time, the news doubted whether the weapons existed at all. And this doubt resembled a denial in practice. As if it were so uncomfortable to admit that at this very moment in Europe an aggressive war had been created out of thin air, one sacrificed a sense of reality in favor of the old familiar way of life. If the war seemed like it might disappear of its own accord, perhaps that was only because it wasn't recognized as war.

On numerous talk shows and on the front pages of newspapers, pundits debated what the people of the Donbas actually wanted out of their *protests* and speculated as to how Russia viewed Ukrainian political events.

In the process, nobody asked the *people of the Donbas*—these inhabitants of Ukraine, a country that before this war had not imposed any great national idea on its own regions—how they actually wanted to live, or whether they even wanted to live at all. Step by step, the Ukrainian Donbas transformed into a battlefield.

But this battlefield was difficult to recognize from afar. Geographical distance functioned like a broken camera lens, blurring the subject of the photograph.

The war, which at first was deemed no more than a *conflict*, developed in opposition to the annexation of Crimea. Crimea was annexed *in a civil manner*. The Donbas was spared any of this so-called civility. Ukraine began to fight back. In the towns and cities of Ukrainian territories controlled by Russia, people began to disappear: they were kidnapped, tortured, forced into silence, or obsessively mobilized into a slapdash army to fight against their own country, against the Ukrainian army, with heavy artillery from Russia.

Already in spring 2014, it was clear that despite rapidly deteriorating living conditions, residents of Russian-occupied cities didn't want to leave their own apartments and houses. Ukrainian society discussed what to make of this. Did it mean that people from the Donbas had become so aligned with Russian propaganda that they wanted to stay in the world it had created? Did it mean that the logic of a decision made by so many—to stay—amounted to a form of political expression? Then presumably they must have expressed themselves through action rather than speech, because the inhabitants of the occupied regions were hardly represented in debates.

In October 2014, I drove to the Donbas with my good friend Pavel Lissianski, the human rights activist and founding member of the Miners' Union, to visit the area for the very first time.

He picked me up in Kharkiv. We planned to go to Debaltseve, the Ukrainian city in Donetsk Oblast, which was partially surrounded by Russian troops and the site of constant skirmishes.

As I write today, just any old day in Berlin, it's hard for me to comprehend that we would decide to set off without any misgivings.

For me it was important to get to know this city and see with my own eyes what was happening. I knew that journalists hardly visited the area. Pavel's colleague lived in Debaltseve before the war and we wanted to pick something up from her abandoned apartment.

War was still no more than a word for me, with the ring of history books and distant, nearly exotic news. I thought, the city is in danger; people's lives are threatened. Even my imagination of danger carried the traces of peacetime, not war.

Now I know that a city—even in the midst of war, fully steeped in war—is capable of preserving little and even bigger islands of peaceful life. Much later, in Kyiv in March 2022, I entered a bakery, open despite the blaring air raid siren, and was greeted with a laughter and warmth that completely shut out the war.

During these recent summer weeks, Russian missiles have attacked Ukrainian cities almost daily. Sometimes I whisper to myself, "Mykolaiv, Vinnytsia, Odessa, Kremenchuk. Kharkiv, Mariupol, Lysychansk." Again and again people are seized on the streets, at bus stops, in their houses. These are city dwellers who can't imagine that their lives, in some new and unbearable manner, can be valued one minute and destroyed the next.

There exists in this war a strange calculation, which obeys no clear logic, that devalues everyday life to the point of negation. In the eyes of those who order an attack on a peaceful city, life in this place has already ceased to exist long before the strike.

Evening was approaching. Pavel was driving very fast through the empty streets. No other cars were heading toward Debaltseve. I wanted to take a picture of this empty road with my big SLR camera. Pavel seemed a little nervous, looking intently ahead. He noticed my camera and asked me in a quiet but emphatic tone, "Please, don't take pictures here, hide the camera. A sniper can catch the glint from your lens and aim to shoot."

That the two of us, hurrying along, immersed in fantasies about the Donbas, could become a target in this war was a new and strange idea to me. I looked with distrust at this landscape entrusted to me. Something was burning up ahead. We quickly approached the blaze. It was a wall of flames—a patch of land and a bush burning as if spontaneously. Not far away there was a black and half-scorched car that seemed to have skidded to the side of the fire.

I stared at the clear evidence of Pavel's concern and hoped it was the remnant of a catastrophe that had long since passed. Pavel patiently explained that apparently this place had fallen under attack only a few hours ago, if not within the last hour.

I felt nauseous and tried to stop looking at the burning car. We drove past. We drove on. For the first time in my life, I felt myself changing with each passing kilometer. Me, taking pictures, reading, writing, thinking, laughing—almost all my traits and abilities lined up and slowly vanished from sight. Nothing mattered anymore; my biography contracted to the fragile assertion of my existence.

These old ideas about myself, so deeply ingrained and somewhat naive, began to thaw, just like the snow woman in the fairy tale: when spring came knocking, the snow woman could no longer resist going out into the sun. Before the eyes of her loving family, she melted drop by drop and disappeared abruptly, without the chance to say goodbye.

Human rights, especially the fundamental right to life, took a palpable form on this journey, like clothing or even a part of my body. And to see the loss of this fundamental right, only because I had traveled to a certain part of my country, led to an almost instinctive search for a replacement.

But it was not to be found. I simply knew it was important to impose this experience on myself. I thought, "There is a chasm between those who have never experienced such a state and those who live in it, who have no say in the matter, who are expected to go on with their lives."

Today, July 16, 2022, I learned from an acquaintance from Mariupol, who now lives in Berlin, that people are returning to this city in ruins. "I can't imagine it," she said with sadness, "we have no water there, no heating, no electricity, nothing! But people return, intent to remain. After everything that happened, with all that has been lost and will never be found again, they return. Doctors are coming to start working in the hospitals. Some live in the rubble and the rest in half-rubble."

When the war first began in the spring of 2014, it was still a child, so fresh that it introduced itself to the world without its own date of birth. Its emergence spread out through time and place over several months. In its first weeks of life, there were days when I kept thinking, maybe I'm wrong and it's not a war after all, just a giant mistake that will soon be fixed and then disappear from reality.

Thursday, February 24

The Beginning

I woke up early this morning to eight missed calls on my cell phone. They were from my parents and some friends. At first, I thought something had happened to my family and that my friends were trying to reach me because my parents had alerted them before me. Then my imagination traveled in another direction, and I envisioned an accident, a dangerous situation in the center of Kyiv, something to warn your friends about. A cold anxiety gripped me. I called my cousin because her beautiful voice, brave and rational, always has a calming effect on me. All she said was, "Kyiv has been shelled. A war has broken out."

Many things have a beginning. When I think about the beginning, I imagine a line drawn very clearly on a white surface. The eye observes the simplicity of this trace of movement—one that is sure to begin somewhere and end somewhere. But I have never been able to imagine the beginning of a war. Strange. I was in the Donbas when war with Russia broke out in 2014. But I had entered the war then, entered into a foggy, opaque zone of violence. I still remember the intense guilt I felt about being a guest in a catastrophe, a guest who could leave at will, because I lived somewhere else.

The war was already there, an intruder, something strange, alien, and insane that had no justification to happen in that place and at that time. Back then, I kept asking people in the Donbas how all this could have started, and I always got different answers.

I think that the beginning of this war in the Donbas was one of the most mythologized moments for the people of Kyiv, precisely because it remained incomprehensible how such an event is born. At that time, in 2014, people in Kyiv said, "The people of the Donbas, those Ukrainian Putin-sympathizers, invited the war to our country." This alleged "invitation" has for some time been considered an explanation for how the absolutely impossible—war with Russia—suddenly became possible after all.

After I got off the phone with my cousin, I paced around my apartment for a while. My head was absolutely blank. I had no idea what to do next. Then my phone rang again. One call followed another, friends came forward with plans to escape, some called to convince themselves we were still alive. I quickly grew tired. I talked a lot, constantly repeating the words "the war." In the meantime, I would look out the window and listen to check if the explosions were approaching. The view from the window was ordinary, but the sounds of the city were strangely muffled—no children yelling, no voices in the air.

Later, I went out and discovered an entirely new environment, an emptiness that I had never seen here, even on the most dangerous days of the Maidan protests.

Sometime later I heard that two children had died from shelling in Kherson Oblast, in the south of the country, and that a total of fifty-seven people had died in the war today. The numbers transformed into something very concrete, as if I had already lost someone myself.

I felt angry at the whole world. I thought, "This has been allowed to happen. It is a crime against everything human, against the great common space where we live and hope for a future."

I'm staying with my parents tonight; our buildings are a five-minute walk apart. I've visited a bomb shelter next to the house, so I know where we'll all go when the shelling comes later.

The war has begun. It is after midnight. I will hardly be able to fall asleep, and there is no point in trying to calculate what has changed forever.

Friday, February 25, Morning

Air Raids

I wake up at seven in the morning to the sirens warning of air raids in progress. My mother is convinced that Russia will not dare to shell the thousand-year-old Saint Sophia Cathedral in our city. She believes that our house, which is in the immediate vicinity of the cathedral, is safe. That's why she decides against going to the bomb shelter. My father is sleeping.

I think if a UNESCO monument could actually stop the Russian army from shelling, this war wouldn't have started in the first place. My head is throbbing with thoughts: Kyiv under fire, abandoned by the whole world, which is ready to sacrifice Ukraine in the hope that it will feed and satiate the aggressor for a while.

Kyiv is being shelled for the first time since the Second World War.

I am struggling with myself. I know that slowly the world is waking up and beginning to see that it's not just about Kyiv and Ukraine. It's about every house, every door—it's about every life in Europe that is threatened as of today.

Tense Silence

All of a sudden, the night is silent. Just an hour ago, around midnight, you could hear the sirens, then distant thunder, perhaps the impact of rockets or artillery. And now—a tense silence.

We should be in the shelter by now, but I've already been there twice today. My parents are tired, and I'm staying in the apartment with them for the night. The idea was that we could rest more comfortably up here, if only for a little bit. We are ready to leave the apartment at a moment's notice and take shelter in the basement of the house.

I find it difficult to collect my thoughts. All of today's distinct experiences crumble into the sensation of many identical days, standing gray next to one another. The space of the city is changing. The walk from my house to the nearest grocery store, which used to take no more than ten minutes, stretches out, the route becoming a long trek.

The fact that the store was open at all was a miracle. I bought apples, vegetables, and buckwheat—but when I returned to the area an hour later, I saw the disappointed faces of two women standing in front of a closed door. Someone said there was another grocery store 500 meters away, down the same street. But it wasn't good news for the two women—500 meters on foot? The sirens are wailing; the streets are emptying of people.

Even time is changing. On the way back from the grocery store, I found out that a kindergarten near the city of Sumy, in the northeast of the country, was shelled today. A kindergarten and a bunker. Seventeen children injured, two seriously. I stopped to lean against the wall of a house. Suddenly the day became infinitely long. Can this war be endured one more minute? Why doesn't the world put an end to it?

It was a spring day. Spots of sunshine played on the sides of houses and the white walls of Saint Sophia Cathedral. The sirens wailed again—the signal to go to the bomb shelter. A good friend of mine,

the artist Nikita Kadan, had lost his credit card, and the two of us walked the streets to find a working ATM.

One journalist had a backpack with him that contained everything he might need in the coming days. We saw some passersby and reporters standing in front of one of the big hotels with their cameras. The second day of the war has proved to be a further step in a recurring sequence.

In the evening I learned that a town in the Luhansk region had been eighty percent destroyed by the Russian army, a beautiful little town that was in Ukrainian-controlled territory. It is called Schastia, meaning "Happiness." The husband of a friend, who was already safe, managed to escape. He left town without a toothbrush, socks, or suitcase.

A car picked him up on the road. He told my friend that as he rode along, he saw the corpses of people lying next to their houses, in front of their doors, and by the small cellars where many Ukrainians store potatoes for the winter. So these were "the people of the Donbas" that Putin claimed he was saving from "genocide."

Happiness no longer exists there. I was in Schastia a few years ago photographing the streets, admiring a hill that looms over the landscape. People in the town spoke Russian and Ukrainian—I had written about them and their strange and comical homemade playgrounds.

Then I fall asleep in this black night after all.

Saturday, February 26

Bomb Shelter

My first night in a bomb shelter. The Telegram channels of the Kyiv government warn that it will be a difficult night and that the Russian military will attack the city. But here in the shelter, it's pretty much empty. Many try to stay at home, hoping that nothing will happen. As of Saturday night there has been a curfew in the city for almost thirty hours. It probably won't be possible to go outside on Sunday.

At the dark entrance to our shelter, I see the silhouettes of residents scurrying past one another. You can always overhear their petty arguments.

Two older shadows pass two younger ones.

"Good evening!" the older shadows say.

"But the evening is not good!" the younger ones protest.

"We wish you a good evening anyway," the older ones say in a triumphant tone, "because we mean well. And we will continue to wish it, to you and to the others!" The shadows disappear into the depths of the cellar.

Every day I watch my father work on his translations. I orient myself in the present because the days offer little structure. At some point I visit my parents. Both of them are not ready to leave Kyiv. They want to stay here until the moment of "our victory," as they say.

My father is a translator. He translates German poetry into Russian. Thanks to my father's translations I fell in love with the work of Paul Celan when I was still a student. For years, since the Maidan Revolution, he has published his translations almost exclusively in Ukraine.

He took part in protests back then. I remember calling him from Berlin and finding out that he was standing with the demonstrators at the parliament building. Then I heard an explosion. Luckily, he wasn't hurt. Now he's in Kyiv. He feels quite weak after a long cold and cannot go to the shelter. Maybe he doesn't want to either. Every day I see how he continues to work on his translations—despite the rocket attacks, despite the danger, or maybe because of it.

As I write, it occurs to me that during the day I saw many smiling people—for example, a woman who was sitting next to two big shopping bags on a park bench. She spoke to me in an absurdly happy voice, saying that she was waiting for her nephew to help her carry the bags home. "I'm so happy to have you standing next to me now, talking to me," she said. "When there are two of us, I'm less afraid of the artillery."

She used to work as a museum guide at Saint Sophia Cathedral, and now she's a pensioner. She is convinced that Ukraine will defeat the Russian invaders: "When I think about the frescoes of Saint Sophia, I believe that Ukraine will be protected by the whole world." She smiled, tears welling in her eyes. "We will win," she said. I didn't know if she was crying more or laughing more, but I felt her courage and admired her.

Is today only the third day of the war? Mariupol: fifty-eight civilians wounded. Kyiv: thirty-five people, including two children. This is far from a complete account. It feels strange to find myself in this broad, unarmed, almost delicate category: "civilians." For war, a category of people is created who live "outside the game." They are shelled, they must endure the shelling, they are injured, but they do not seem to be able to give an adequate response to it.

I don't believe this to be the case. There is something hidden in the smiles that I saw several times today—a secret weapon, an uncanny one. I must try to sleep at last and reach my apartment in the morning. Having breakfast in my own kitchen—that would be an enormous pleasure!

Sunday, February 27

An Extinguished City

Normally, the many brightly lit windows in Kyiv warm the city's cold February days. The lights have something secret and private, while at the same time cozy about them. But now the lights of the city have gone out. People are afraid of Russian missiles and artillery fire. I tape my windows shut so that they won't shatter in case of shelling. I go out on the balcony to see if my apartment is dark enough. I place only one lamp in each room—they hardly give off any light where they stand on the floor. It's difficult for me to find my way around the apartment, but I'm trying to discover a new form of comfort.

The sirens that warn of air strikes wail with a long signal that is somewhat reminiscent of the playful sounds elephants use to communicate. In Kyiv, the wailing of sirens is also a form of communication, but the message is always the same: "Hide, as best you can!"

When dawn came, I decided for some reason to clean my apartment. I thought, "Right now you have to stick to the plan, to the usual routines." From the outside, my apartment is almost black, with its empty, dark windows greeting all the other dark and empty apartments in the city.

The darkness is frightening, but at the same time I sense that the city has decided to defend itself. On official Telegram channels, I read about so-called diversionary groups, Russian units moving into Kyiv as a vanguard. Like terrorists. Their goal is to destabilize the city, carry out attacks on politicians, and ultimately take over Kyiv. One such group appears to have shot at the car of two women who had decided to flee the city with their children this morning. The women and their children died.

My thoughts become as dark as the windows of my apartment. While cleaning, I thought that when I write this diary, I should make a joke about housekeeping during war. My tip would be: "Cleanliness is a must in a dark room with taped windows—if you were going to do it earlier and are now on the verge of tears, go ahead and mop your apartment anyway. True, you will not see anything, and the apartment may not get much cleaner, but following procedure and implementing plans is more important."

The fourth day of the war is over. Half the city is resisting the normalization of violence that knocks on every door. War also tests us to see if we have even a touch of compassion for those sent here to kill. Since the war began, sixteen children have been murdered across the country. In my town, nine "civilians" (I hate that word more and more) have died so far, and forty-seven have been injured, including three children.

The destruction of the small town of Schastia, "Happiness," in northeastern Ukraine, began with the shelling of an electrical station. At some point it was destroyed—the lights went out, water, heating. In distress, people, especially elderly residents, ventured outside for water and food. At this very moment the soldiers attacked with artillery and rockets. A bus with fleeing people was fired upon. There are no journalists in this area at the moment. No one counts the injured, the murdered. Who will describe what Putin has done to the Donbas since the beginning of the war, since his operation to "Protect the people of the Donbas from Ukrainian fascists"?

By occupying these territories and waging information warfare, Putin has managed to isolate this region from the world. The occupied territories have not been observed by a human rights organization since 2014, and now the Russian army is once again showing how little it values the lives of these people.

From the news, I learn that the Regional History Museum—in the settlement of Ivankiv, in Kyiv Oblast—was destroyed. In it were the works of Maria Prymachenko, one of the most famous twentieth-century artists in Ukraine. A joint exhibition of my photographs and her paintings had been planned for the fall—a great honor for me. I am sure that somehow, somewhere, this exhibition will take place.

Monday, February 28

Our New Vulnerability

It's a sunny spring day that, like the last three, ends in darkness. I sit in the darkened apartment. Some lights burn, but those lights are dim and hidden. I read the news that Mariupol is bravely resisting Russian troops, but is largely in darkness itself. Russia is attacking infrastructure as planned, firing rockets at a city where people are already living without electricity. Fighting continues around Kyiv.

But my thoughts are with Kharkiv. I see the images of apartment blocks destroyed by rockets and mortar shells, and I know that today Putin's army murdered nine people, including three children, in this Russian-speaking city resisting occupation. Thirty-seven people are injured, eighty-seven apartment buildings ruined. I live in Kyiv in a similar building—a vulnerable refuge, my own apartment, where I always feel so good. Even now! Even now!

This war is demonstrating our new level of vulnerability to the world. Almost all the pharmacies are closed. Electricity, water, and heating are under constant threat of failure. The wounds are getting bigger. But sometimes a little voice comes to whisper in my ear, constantly repeating: "They keep fighting, we keep fighting." Then the wounds heal faster.

The city's public spaces, squares, and streets are empty. The horizon is suddenly closer. The Kyiv hills, the asphalt, the courtyards of the buildings—everything is invited to join the war.

At noon I decided to go for a walk: on the fifth day of the war, when the curfew lifted, I accompanied a German friend, who could not stay in Kyiv, to the train station. We were going to take the subway first. Inspired and almost drunk on the idea that the subway in Kyiv was working again, we walked to the Golden Gate station. Then, at the entrance, we learned that this station was only in use as a shelter.

(As I write this, sirens shatter the silence. It is 2:30 in the morning, and I decide to stay where I am and finish this diary entry.)

So we had to walk to the train station—a journey of twenty-five minutes, which for me was like wandering into a vast new reality. Since the beginning of the war, I have not visited Shevchenko Boulevard, a wide street that leads to the station. We walked along the street, and every house, every intersection carried something new within it, a new language, a new narrative about our shared reality. The city looked peaceful. The sun's rays made this image even more jarring. We quickly said goodbye, and I strolled back alone.

I wanted to cross the street so I could swing by the old botanical garden. Suddenly I saw a pile of metal on the side of the road—a shot-up, deformed car—then a second one nearby, plus a broken promotional sign, its shattered glass, metal, and plastic lying on the ground. The botanical garden was wiped from my mind. What remained was the unbearable realization that this war, this unimaginable, illogical, criminal war, was still going on after all.

At about the same time, peaceful residents of Berdyansk, a city in the south of the country, gathered in front of their city hall, which was occupied by Putin's army and guarded by armed soldiers. The women shouted at the soldiers in Russian, "How can you look your mothers in the face? You brought war and slaughter to our land! Shame on you!" Old people were also in the crowd—they were not afraid. The soldiers looked demoralized, replying, "We came to protect you!"

The women resisted. They continued to protest. "We were never in danger here," they said. "There was no threat to us here before you came. Now, with you, because of you, we are in the greatest danger." Then came curses, which have a rich expression in the Ukrainian and Russian languages.

This ability of the residents of Berdyansk to go on fighting, to approach the soldiers unarmed and shout the truth in their faces, even when the city has almost fallen into Putin's hands—this promises a lot. It is hope itself.

Not a Minute More of This War!

Russia has announced that it will bomb the area around Saint Sophia Cathedral, which is a UNESCO World Heritage Site. Not the cathedral itself, Russia says, but a secret service building in the immediate vicinity. If that happens, the cathedral will certainly be hit as well.

My parents and I live next to Saint Sophia. I had decided to spend the curfew at their place tonight. Meanwhile, our worried neighbors went to the shelters. Most residents have long since chosen a shelter for themselves. They try to do everything they can to feel comfortable there.

I'm in an absurdly good mood. But this good mood is of little use, superimposed as it is on a deep sense of worry and sorrow. Our apartment is in darkness. I learn that the western bank of the Dnieper River in Kyiv is under fire, including Zhulany Airport, which is on the eastern bank, fairly close to the city center. The number of casualties is unclear.

However, all my thoughts are with Kharkiv. I see videos of burning streets on Twitter and Telegram, and I know from acquaintances in the city that people have remained in shelters there for days. The well-known economics professor Oleh Amosov, chair of the Department of Economic Theory and Public Finance at the Kharkiv Regional Institute of Public Administration, died of injuries after an attack. This is the second day the city has been bombed. My thoughts are now with two cities in the Luhansk and Donetsk districts: Severodonetsk and Volnovakha.

I was often on the road in and around Severodonetsk. Even when this city was at the center of the Russian invasion, from 2014 to 2016, it had a cheerful appearance. Cafes and restaurants were open almost all night, and the crowd there always amused me: Western-dressed and sometimes arrogant representatives of the international press mingled with spoiled and outlandishly styled young women from Donetsk, who had decided to spend a few months in their home region on the escape route to central Ukraine.

Now, Severodonetsk and Volnovakha are being completely destroyed. There is no electricity and no water, and Russian mortar shells are falling from the sky. All those who try to find food or water, for their families or themselves, are dying in the streets.

I would really like to scream. Save these people! Journalists who have experienced wartime in the Donbas and lived in the mostly peaceful Severodonetsk, get outraged! We need humanitarian corridors and zones where men, women, and children can save themselves. Put even more pressure on Russia. Putin has sentenced these cities to death. Russia is destroying the Donbas. No, that sounds wrong. "Donbas" is just a word, and this word says very little. You have to save the inhabitants of these cities. Actually, you have to save everything, the whole country. Urgently.

Now I'm trying to understand where my good mood comes from. It is the sixth day of the war, which I feel has already lasted fifty years. Earlier today I drank a cappuccino for the first time since the invasion began.

I went for a walk to breathe some fresh air on this first day of spring and maybe do some shopping. Knowing that many supermarket shelves were already empty, I decided to visit a shopping mall that had recently opened not far from us. What a joy it was to be there! The supermarket is deep underground, and everyone walked past the shelves with a slowness that hasn't been seen in Kyiv for six days.

An elderly lady stood next to the coffee machine. Her shopping bag was small and half empty. Then suddenly I saw a young, fashionably dressed woman approach the lady and press a bill into her hand. The lady was surprised and said, "But I didn't ask for anything. I have everything!" A young man came up to her; he also slipped her a bill. The elderly lady resisted at first, but then she seemed happy and grateful.

On the way back, I took a picture of an old man sitting alone on a bench in a park. He needed to talk to me. His wife is ill, he told me, and he is taking care of her. He wants to take care of her until tomorrow—then he will join the Kyiv Territorial Defense. He and his wife are sixty-six years old.

In his youth he served in the military. He said he no longer wants to just watch as our city suffers from constant shelling. I started thanking him—I couldn't stop. I used all kinds of words and phrases of thanks, but I wished I could add more to these expressions, as if that would prevent this elderly man who is caring for his sick wife from risking his life.

I await a solution. A solution must be found, discovered, worked out. The aggression must stop. Not a minute more of this war!

The sirens are wailing again. My father sits in the next room learning English vocabulary. A good friend of mine calls and says that perhaps the last evacuation bus will leave from a Kyiv synagogue tomorrow. Maybe I can try to convince my parents to leave the city after all. In vain I try to talk to them about it. We are needed here more than before, they say. It is not the time to leave Kyiv. I agree and try to sleep a few more hours. We'll stay and see what happens.

Time to Be Brave

The city is sinking into a spring fog, but it's still cold. Since yesterday, here, in the center of Kyiv, you can tell a story about the war on every street corner. Almost every intersection is guarded day and night by armed members of the Territorial Defense. There are more groups of saboteurs in the city, more violence. I look with relief into the eyes of the men and women of the defense. In one of the faces yesterday I recognized with amazement a barista who was popular in our neighborhood for painting beautiful swans with the milk foam of the coffees he served.

Outside, I hear another explosion. At such times, fear overtakes me, and I think about how to save myself and the people I love from this situation. It is always a chain of relationships that I consider—it is not only my father and mother, but also my aunt lying at home, sick and weak. And it is not only my aunt, but also her whole family. And then I see other connections that are hard to break.

The answer is to keep everyone safe, not just individuals. Now is the time to act bravely and find strong, effective means against the aggressor. In my imagination, a hundred variations are already playing out for how all this can stop, how the war will end, at this specific moment. Then I imagine how we would dance in the streets.

My day has been long and feels like it has several days locked up in it. The images of empty streets filled with droning silence float before my eyes. I have experienced and seen a lot today, even visited an exhibition.

The artist Nikita Kadan, a friend of mine, has moved to a small private gallery located in a basement. Really, it's not so much a gallery anymore but a shelter and apartment for artists and their friends. Yesterday Nikita called and invited me to a group show he was putting together from the gallery's collection. I was about to go meet him, but then the sirens howled once again, and I had to stay inside.

So the exhibition "opened" yesterday without visitors and was supposed to close the same day. But then he decided that it would stay open for me to visit today. In peacetime I would be unspeakably happy about such an honor and even now, as the air over the city turns ominous, I notice the traces of joy that this feeling leaves on the sandy foundation of my restlessness. Nikita titled the exhibition "Fear."

There was another air raid warning, and this afternoon when I was finally about to leave, my father called and asked me to take him along. Somewhat reluctantly, I agreed. And then the three of us went! My father, my mother, and me.

Our journey was long. The city seemed strange. We must have walked more than half an hour—it was my longest walk since the beginning of the war.

The way back was shorter, short like a jump.

I enjoyed the exhibition very much. I am still thinking about the pictures and this extraordinary chance to look at them in the midst of war and seal them in my memory.

What can art do? What can a single voice achieve? What can the courage of resistance win, and what is the point of resistance in the first place? I keep getting emails and messages telling me to be a pacifist. Ukrainians have never provoked a war, never wanted or supported a war. The values of pacifism are among the most important values of my country. I grew up with a saying: "The most important thing is that there be no war." The shuddering memories of the Second World War, some of which took place on Ukrainian soil, are still very much alive.

However, there are values much bigger than Ukraine that need to be defended. There are situations where resistance means salvation. And it is not about self-help—it is about rescuing ourselves from a much greater violence, from a much more terrible war. I hope that every day more people understand this, wake up, and put an end to this violence.

DAY 8   *Thursday, March 3*

Alienation

It is the evening of the eighth day of the war, and I am looking at
photos of empty streets taken with my cell phone and my small digital
camera. When I photograph the streets, I try not to show faces. I feel
that anything with a face, anything that could be identified, would
rather remain in shadow.

A week has passed since the invasion began. No matter how hard I
try, I can't remember any particular news or event from that first day,
even though I've been carefully writing down important news in a
notebook. Have I become accustomed to these events? Today, a sense
of alienation came over me: I felt at a strange remove from everything.
I try to place the moment when this strange state began, and I find it.

In the morning, still in bed, I saw a video clip of a Russian soldier operating a Grad system. Grad means "hail," and the weapon is

a multiple-rocket launcher that the Russian army has been using to attack peaceful districts in Ukrainian cities. The soldier in the video was crying. He said he wanted to apologize to his young daughter because he may be guilty of killing children in Ukraine.

Then he addressed other members of the Russian military and asked them to disobey orders and not come to Ukraine. I watched him cry again and again. Then I saw pictures of the destroyed apartment buildings in Chernihiv. These two pieces of news merged in my mind. Many friends of my mother live in Chernihiv. They were always proud of this small and clean city. I know that now, as I write this, the city is being shelled. An oil depot has been set on fire, and this small city, a favorite vacation destination for many of my friends, now threatens ecological disaster across the country. Danger comes from the sky. Houses are bombed. One begins to count the victims.

Over the past few days, I have been wondering how obedience works. The soldier in the video cried only after he had obeyed his orders. That was already too late. This war can be stopped if the orders to shell homes are ignored—by soldiers, even by generals. I know that sounds naive. But on such a day, naivete is the best bunker. Its walls are not very thick, but it is deep enough.

So far, thirty-three dead residents have been found in the rubble of Chernihiv. Today feels particularly ominous. Almost every half hour an explosion can be heard outside in the streets.

A young woman living in the house next door is trying to rescue pets that were left behind. Perhaps the owners couldn't take their pets when they fled. She finds warm, comfortable places for the animals and gives them food. An elderly lady who lives across the street goes shopping several times throughout the day so that her neighbors can stay home in safety.

A well-known teacher, eighty-six years old, spends most nights in the basement of a school next to her house. Today she recorded a video. In a particularly noble Kyiv accent from an almost forgotten past, she addressed the women of Russia: "Do not let your sons go to war."

It is snowing, the air is damp and cold, and it seems to me that I can no longer get close to my own city, the place where I live, whose events I witness. I resist violence more than I used to. I resist acknowledging that the war is going on, that it has been allowed, that it has been tolerated.

I can try to accept it. I can try to face reality. But then I ask myself, "How will we all be able to live with the thought that these war crimes took place, every day, on our doorsteps?" At some point we will have to forgive ourselves that this inhumanity was even possible. But to really be able to do that, you have to protect the skies in my country. The bombing of homes must finally stop.

Friday, March 4

"Follow me on Instagram"

During the night, I read that in the city of Enerhodar the nuclear power plant was attacked. I had a fragmented night of sleep. There were wounded employees who could not be evacuated for hours and bled to death. The fire department was shot at. Three employees died, and in the morning the wounded were evacuated. The nuclear power plant in Chernobyl is occupied, too, and for ten days the employees haven't been able to go home. It is very dangerous to stay there for so long. The news was unbearable. I fell asleep again.

This morning, I woke up quite early in a bright mood and with the feeling that this sunny day had something to offer me. I wanted to get out on the street earlier than I did yesterday, to see what was happening in the city. Little was left of the melancholy I felt yesterday. Then I discovered the reason for this change: I no longer believe in the war!

"It simply can't be," I thought. "It isn't true. What neighboring country bombs a city to rubble in the twenty-first century?"

The invaders have no political plan. They have no ability to come to power here permanently. You can't occupy this country. It is unrealistic. The war is a dream, a dictator's fantasy.

I wanted to see if the little store next to our house still had bread. I haven't been able to get bread since the third day of the war—it's usually sold out.

The store was full. With some amazement, I discovered a group whom I took to be foreign military personnel. They spoke English and needed help translating. Then I realized that they weren't soldiers. Rather, they were unarmed but well-protected escorts of a war photographer who was also shopping in the store. I tried to help her choose a detergent. The small group exuded enthusiasm, humor, and inspiration. My mood suddenly darkened. One of the three escorts proudly said to me, "Do you know who stands next to you? This is one of the best photographers in the world!"

The photographer laughed and shrugged it off. "Please," she said. "I'm embarrassed." Then she told me her name. I can't remember it. I've been having a hard time concentrating lately. Then she said, "You can follow me on Instagram." The group bought a lot of detergent, almost everything in the store. I told them, "Good to have you with us," and said goodbye. Uneasiness quickly washed over me; I realized that it isn't a good sign when a well-known war photographer and her entourage set up shop in your city.

On a side street, I came upon a bakery that used to be quite expensive before the war. It was open for business. Nice white bread lined the shelves, and they also had coffee. It was a miracle. Men and women stood there drinking cappuccinos and discussing whether or not to stay in town. One older man who looked like a geography professor said he would not leave the city until he had to spend every day and every night in the shelter. The bystanders tried to convince him that it would never come to that: "Kyiv is a holy city after all. The city would never permit it!"

Afterward, I found an empty street to take a photo. As I took the camera out of my pocket, a car stopped next to me. Four armed men jumped out. They took my cell phone, searched my bag, and asked me who I worked for. It took a few minutes. Then they excused themselves, all four of them looking nervous and tired.

One of them said, "I understand it's your job, but please don't take pictures! You can see what they're doing." He meant the attackers. "They are shelling residential buildings now; they are using everything as a target. It seems unimaginable, but it is happening. There are eight hundred and forty injured children."

My photos are harmless, I thought. I'm being careful, after all. Besides, our city is photographed all the time anyway. But maybe I need to be even more careful.

I thought about that number: eight hundred and forty injured children. Our sky must be protected! The news repeated that number, but it's hard to really grasp.

I am sure that the world will not continue to sit by and watch this happen—I can't watch it anymore myself. Do not be afraid of this criminal. He acts without logic. If you protect the sky here, you will save so much!

At home I got a message that a friend of mine was looking for her acquaintance, an artist who lives with his wife and two small children in Mariupol and has been unreachable for three days. His last message to her was, "If you know anyone who works for Western media, tell them that we are nearly out of water here, out of food, out of medicine, and now the electricity has been cut off. They are destroying our town. Sartana, a village, keeps getting shelled. I don't know if there is anything left. So many victims." I know that Mariupol—a Russian-speaking town in the Donbas with beautiful little houses from the nineteenth century—is in darkness, without electricity.

Eight hundred and forty. This is no longer just war—this is mass murder of the defenseless. The Ukrainian army is protecting us, but the Russian tanks, artillery, and rifles are aiming at peaceful people, at women and children, at residential houses! It is time to stop being afraid and close the sky.

In Russia, independent media outlets are either shut down or censored. What remains is the opposition newspaper *Republic*, which is trying to survive despite censorship. One headline read, "We are trying to restore the Soviet Empire. But there is little chance of that." That's how some Russian oppositionists think: they fear there is a chance, albeit a slim one, that the empire might be restored. In reality, there is no chance at all.

"A great beauty"

Tenth day of war. I learned how to darken the windows of my apartment with thin blankets so that a soft, muted light fills the interior. I remember the first morning of the war. Everything was normal—I woke up a little late, at nine, and saw a series of messages on my cell phone from friends and acquaintances: "Please, answer the phone!" Again and again the same message.

The catastrophe must be represented—only as part of a narrative can it be recognized as catastrophic. Communication can offer a way out. The hope is that once everything is reported and everyone is informed, those who receive our message can end the catastrophe.

Our skies are still open to military planes and bombs, which means our cities full of men, women, children, homes, and museums are still under threat of bombardment. This morning I read that in Bila

Tserkva, one of the most beautiful towns in Kyiv Oblast, an airstrike destroyed twenty residential houses. Bila Tserkva means "White Church." The number of victims is still unclear. Fortunately, a timely evacuation was organized.

A friend from Zaporizhzhia, in southeastern Ukraine, called me and explained with excitement that humanitarian aid in the form of food and medicine was finally being delivered to Mariupol. His neighbor heard from supposedly reliable sources that this war will be over as early as mid-March. Laughing, I said goodbye.

I remember an elegant lady I saw earlier today. She was wearing a long black coat with fur trim, high boots, and a hat, and was waiting in line in front of a pharmacy. My mother had also waited—for five hours—in this line. The air was cold, so my mother paced around to warm up. At some point I joined her. No one else in line, including my mother and me, looked particularly fancy. Businesslike, maybe, but still dressed somewhat casually. So the lady in the fur coat stood out a little. Her eyes looked worried, but for me, at that moment, she was a kind of beacon—one that reminded me, and perhaps the others in line, of a bygone Kyiv.

We decided to go for a little walk. On the way back, I met a young man in front of my house and spoke with him. He said his name was Kirill. He was apparently part of the Kyiv nightclub scene, which has developed rapidly in recent years. Now, nearly every day, he makes an almost unimaginable trek from the eastern bank of the Dnieper across to the western bank, to cook food in the kitchen of a restaurant for people in bomb shelters and in the Kyiv Territorial Defense. When time permits, he concerns himself with art, music, and shamanism. Our conversation was a little strange.

"It has become very difficult to have faith in others," he said. "As it turns out, they can suddenly throw bombs at other people and think they're right about it, too." He looked directly at me. "Do you happen to be a journalist who could write about me?" I replied that maybe I could write about our meeting, in this diary. "Then I want to say"—he seemed very passionate now—"that everything that is happening at the moment is a great beauty. I don't want to hide. Feel free to take my picture if you like."

I must have looked at him in amazement because he launched into an explanation. "People are acting better than they typically do right now, and our country..." His thought trailed off. Then he said, "Everything is changing, even internationally." His good humor mixed with my bitterness. I began to laugh.

When I got home that evening, I learned that the food and medicine that was supposed to go to Mariupol never reached the city. Because of continual shelling, the humanitarian corridor could not be opened. Two people from my circle of friends—an artist and an art historian—live outside Mariupol. They have been unreachable for four days. News about Mariupol on Telegram channels is becoming less frequent.

I know from a close friend that the village of Horynka, near the forest of Pushcha, was badly damaged. The number of victims is unknown, and my friend's uncle is currently hiding in a basement. We're searching for evacuation routes for him.

It is difficult for me to finish this text. The war continues, but the fear of the aggressor—which amounts to respect—must come to an end. I get letters from my German friends, who write: "Save yourself! Putin does not tolerate any losses. He has a reputation for destroying everything." I wonder what they mean by that. How did he get such a reputation? What does it mean that he doesn't want to lose? What does it mean for the whole world?

Sunday, March 6

"It's 3:30 p.m. and we're still alive"

These days it's hard to grasp tomorrow. Tomorrow seems an eternity away, as if it were happening on another planet. One can imagine tomorrow in theory, but not as a moment in one's own passage of time—only as a story one tells oneself.

I woke up with the feeling that it's good I am in Kyiv and have not left the city yet. I wanted to go out in the street right away, but I couldn't because I still had a lot to do. After all, it was a special day. I had arranged to see a colleague, Polina Veller, a young artist and designer from Kyiv, whom I met with recently in a grocery store.

Polina is staying in Kyiv with her husband and little daughter who can hardly tolerate long trips, so they needed to find a place to sleep. When the war began, Polina started using plastic cable ties in the colors of the Ukrainian flag to make masks that look like strange veils.

We decided to meet midway between our apartments and play at fashion photography. We were focused on the absurdity of our activity, the absurdity of basically any activity in the face of current events, and the idea that you keep going despite it all.

A man approached and said that he'd noticed me looking at the street through the viewfinder of my camera. "I'd like to warn you," he said, "that in these times you can get shot in the head for that!" I replied in amazement that I was just doing my job as a journalist. Then he said, "In that case, maybe it's fine." Only when he was gone did I realize that he had been threatening me. Tension grows in the city. A camera symbolizes an eye that can be aimed at anyone. Photography becomes even more suspicious than usual.

A few pedestrians watched and failed to hide their surprise as Polina posed with her mask for my pictures.

I walked back home. The little camera I like to carry with me suddenly felt like a shield protecting me against vague suspicion. I thought about the power of the photographic image—a power that can serve as a witness to history, but is feared for precisely this reason.

On the way back, I saw many young faces. A group of volunteers were busy collecting food to be distributed over the next few weeks. Can you believe that just two weeks ago everything in Kyiv was functioning normally—cafes, restaurants, shops, and grocery stores? People walked the streets, sometimes without a destination, just strolling to familiar or popular places.

One peculiarity of war is this new, utilitarian form of walking. To go out, you have to have something important in mind—you reach your destination, and then you go straight back. Almost all destinations are linked to food or medicine in some way.

A lot happened today. In the evening, I learned that a friend of mine was evacuated from the small town of Irpin, northwest of Kyiv. Along the way she lost her dog, who was frightened by the explosions and ran off. She saw with her own eyes how women with children were being targeted as they tried to board an evacuation bus. Then something heavy crashed to the ground not far from them, a bomb perhaps, and everyone on the bus was knocked over. My friend told me, "I want to survive so I can describe this evacuation in The Hague." A photographer friend of mine was also evacuated from Irpin. For some incomprehensible reason he and others trying to get on the bus were shot at. A bullet hit him in the upper arm.

Some were murdered during the evacuation. The estimate so far is six women and children, but the exact number of victims and the injured is still being verified. A poet friend of my parents stayed in Irpin with his wife, since they take care of his elderly mother who can no longer stand up. When my parents called them, his wife started to scream: "Leave us alone! Don't you see what's happening here?" A few hours later, my parents received a text message from her: "It's 3:30 p.m. and we are still alive."

Humanitarian aid still hasn't reached Mariupol, in the south. We don't know how many victims the city has to mourn. The people there still don't have medicine, food, water, or electricity. They are shelled every day. The head of the municipal council of Hostomel, an embattled village northwest of Kyiv, was deliberately killed because, despite the danger, he had continued to distribute bread and medicine for his community. Hostomel is partially occupied. As of today, Putin has announced further attacks throughout the country. He intends to bomb military infrastructure, which is often next to houses and residential settlements. Some people cannot leave because they take care of relatives who cannot, or will not, flee.

These crimes are happening before the eyes of the whole world. People even tell us in advance who tomorrow's victims will be—like in a prison where everyone is already sentenced to death. But this is only the vision of a petty dictator. We are fighting back. We are trying to help one another and not allow any more senseless deaths.

Yet the world at large seems watch these criminal proclamations with a strange patience. International fear of the dictator reigns. Perhaps some people think that if they don't challenge or provoke him, he won't do anything worse. This caution has already cost so much, and it is getting more expensive every minute. We are all victims, but we are also all partly responsible. We cannot wait any longer! Stop this violence!

DAY 12   *Monday, March 7*

A Way of Life That Swallows Up Everything

I'm having a hard time concentrating today and keeping track of what's happening. The war is ongoing, and I am somewhere in the midst of events that are developing chaotically around me. Peacetime seems unattainably far away. New laws and a new reality are unfolding.

I receive a utility bill for my Kyiv apartment. It is accompanied by a Telegram message that sounds like an apology: "We are writing to you with a request. If your financial means allow it under current circumstances, please pay the utilities. Many Kyiv utility workers joined the Ukrainian army and are now fighting for our freedom. But it is still important to settle the bill."

The same text was posted on the Kyiv municipal utilities website. I recalled some of the faces of the employees of these companies, faces so incompatible with war. Everywhere I look, I see war: a total, all-encompassing way of life that swallows up everything.

During the day I met an old friend, an historian and sociologist who lives far away, on the other side of the city. Early in the morning he went to the city center to help a friend's mother evacuate.

She was waiting at the station with four small bags and a suitcase, even though my friend begged her to bring just one. I heard her voice on the phone, crying as she described the difficulties of boarding the crowded train, crying again as she explained she had made it onto the train car and had just found a seat.

My friend can't find peace. Yesterday, he helped his uncle escape a partially burned-out village near Kyiv, and now he's tracking down the phone numbers of those who remain. In this quaint little village called Horenka, the pharmacy was shelled and destroyed on February 28, the fifth day of the war. Then, at the beginning of March, Horenka was repeatedly the target of Grad rockets.

As for most of the houses, only a few load-bearing walls remain. I had often visited this town, but now I don't recognize anything from these photographs documenting ruins.

In Zaporizhzhia Oblast, two postal workers were shot dead in a mail truck while trying to deliver pensions to elderly people who could no longer collect the money themselves. I can picture this Ukrainian mail truck very clearly—several times, when I was young, I saw postal workers deliver my grandma's pension to her. She was weak and couldn't leave the apartment, but she was very proud when this small sum of money—rapidly losing value through inflation—was handed to her personally. She became fast friends with one of the postal workers, always sharing a little polite chitchat. In my memory, they both looked happy in that moment—two women giving each other the gift of their presence and support.

The delivery of the pension was a human gesture, a symbol of welfare—more than simply welfare from the corrupt state. I can imagine a mail truck, but to picture such a truck under fire is beyond my imagination.

I hope that everyone who delivers something, who provides care for someone, will reach their destination safely tomorrow. That's my wish for March 8. I will be keeping in mind those who despite the grave danger, continue to take care of the people of this country as they try to reach someone.

Tuesday, March 8

"The night is still young"

When I entered today's date into my Word document, it looked suspicious and unnatural. Time goes on—one day after the other, the sequence is predictable, after light comes the night. At the same time, almost everything that happens is contrary to the state of life—I don't want to say "contrary to normality." I search for a more appropriate word but cannot find it. This word should describe a total destruction but at the same time keep open the possibility that so much can still be saved.

Today I gave an interview to a journalist. I was a little late, but we still had time to talk. Some questions were uncomfortable, but I couldn't stop answering them. The journalist asked me: "When I listen to you, it sounds as if everything around you is functioning normally, you talk about the people in the streets. . . . How do you even fathom that the war is really here?"

Her question tormented me. As I searched for an answer, I noticed how I began to justify myself, how I tried to prove the catastrophe by describing the war—as if one could still doubt that war is here. But you can hardly describe the catastrophe at this scale. All you can do is stop it. That is the only thing to be done.

I ran into some women outside the pharmacy. When I told them that I'm writing a public diary, most of them said the same thing: "The world has to help us close the sky over Ukraine. Can you pass it on?"

In front of me I see the masked faces of Russian pilots who were lucky enough to survive their planes being shot down before they were then arrested. There are video clips on Telegram from their interrogations. We don't know who we drop the bombs on," they say. "We just get coordinates for the air strikes, and then we follow orders."

A friend who was evacuated from a small town outside Kyiv told me that peaceful people are being taken prisoner in the parts of town controlled by Putin's army. The Russian army breaks into private homes and takes entire families away. How often does this happen? How many have already been taken prisoner in this barbaric way? Where are these people now?

The occupied districts, villages, and small towns are often the least visible. They get bogged down quickly by a news blockade. Often there is no electricity in these areas, so it is hard to keep in contact with the people there. Louder voices reporting other tragedies flood the airwaves. You want to listen because it's a form of contact, because you can offer help directly—or at least hope to help.

Putin demands the annexation of the occupied territories in the Donbas and Luhansk Oblast. All the villages and cities that fall to his power will be silenced by the occupiers. Even under the circumstances of terror that Ukraine is living through right now, it is unimaginable to allow the Russian army to keep swallowing villages and cities.

When I left my apartment today, I saw an empty street. No cars, no pedestrians. At such moments Kyiv seems like a city that has yet to be inhabited—a city without a present, with only a past and a future. A few steps farther, I saw two people on the street holding flowers in their hands. This is one tradition that has broken through the cold wall of war: women are gifted flowers on March 8, International Women's Day. Outside the pharmacy, I spotted many women with flowers, prepared for a long wait in the cold. A car had stopped at the pharmacy, and someone had gotten out and handed flowers to those in line.

This big city goes on living. There are still flowers somewhere. In closed restaurants, food is cooked for the Territorial Defense of Kyiv. The elderly ladies and gentlemen who are actors in a theater group for seniors stay together. A few years ago, my mother took over as the director of this self-organized theater group, which calls itself "The Night Is Still Young."

Now these elderly actors and actresses volunteer to defend Kyiv. They don't want to leave the city. I must add that these talented people know hundreds of poems by heart and sing beautifully. Sometimes they write the scripts for their productions—even if some of them still find it difficult to step onto the stage. Now they don't just want to help, they want to join the Territorial Defense. I try to imagine this and suddenly think, "With such defenders, nothing can happen to this city."

Wednesday, March 9

A Blemish in the Landscape

Today I walked with almost no trace of fear along Landscape Alley, one of the most beautiful and busy streets in Kyiv. It's an avenue with a magnificent view of the left bank of the Dnieper River and the city's residential districts. This avenue is also called Sculpture Park. It runs past old Kyiv houses and down to the history museum. On most days since the beginning of the war, Landscape Alley has been almost completely deserted. It seems to have become too anxiety-inducing because the street is so open and unprotected.

Nowadays, the avenue is only visited by those who stayed in Kyiv and live nearby and those who walk their dogs. Although there are very few pedestrians, it is no longer completely empty like it was at the start of the war.

The sirens announced an air raid, but I stopped anyway and

enjoyed the view. Then I noticed a large white cloud of smoke in the distance. Something was burning. I searched on Telegram but found no clue as to what it could be.

It was an idyllic landscape, except for the distant sign of fire like a single blemish. Then I heard a man's sobbing voice approach me.

This man, who looked homeless, was walking down the avenue with an old backpack. He had wrapped plastic bags around his shoes to warm his feet and keep them dry. In his hand, he carried a small, half-empty vodka bottle. As he walked, he spoke very loudly into his cell phone, repeatedly asking after someone. With each answer, he broke into sobs, like a child, over and over again. I understood through fragments that he was talking about an evacuation. I caught up with him and slipped him some money, which he accepted without interrupting his conversation.

Wherever I go, I see mostly polite, caring, calm faces: grocery store employees, volunteers, soldiers, and members of the Territorial Defense. I also meet exhausted, sad people, especially doctors. But this was the first time since the beginning of the war that I'd seen someone crying. At least that's what I was thinking at the moment.

I read on Telegram that some residents of the embattled city of Chernihiv had fled on foot. Maybe acquaintances or friends of the crying man were among them? They evacuated on their own without waiting for transport. Then they were shot at outside the city. Some of them were killed. In Mariupol, a children's hospital and a maternity clinic were destroyed by an air strike. People in Mariupol still don't have electricity, water, food, or medicine, and many have died in the attacks. More and more details of the war stand dimly before the doors of my memory.

I went to the city center where a small outdoor concert was taking place. I still heard the loud sobbing of the homeless man in my ears. "Here in Kyiv," I thought, "you get used to watching the endless days of war with tearless eyes—trying to do something every hour, every minute, to organize something, to help someone." For example, a small store selling bread and eggs next to my house is still open, only because an employee decided to sleep there every night.

A doctor told me today that she hasn't returned home since going in to work on February 24. For the Kyiv residents who continue to stand at grocery store checkouts or care for the sick, driving to work has become too risky and unsafe. Whatever still functions in this city of three million people only does so because someone doesn't sleep in their own bed for days on end, helping others almost around the clock.

Thursday, March 10

Illusions

A day feels like a self-contained unit in a diary. An entry feeds the illusion that conclusions can be drawn—the illusion of a logical narrative.

This war takes shape through many such illusions. For example, it had a preface that preceded the actual attacks: Russian divisions gathered at the border of Ukraine; politicians spoke of war; diplomats left the country. The war followed upon this expectation, this prediction, like a play where the plot is told in a preamble, as a prophecy to be fulfilled.

I'm still struggling to imagine what happens when you learn that war is knocking at the door, a war whose cycle will terrorize peaceful cities with bombs and murder thousands of people. Today, the news in Ukraine said that civilian casualties are much higher than military casualties.

I suspect that before the war started, even the politicians who predicted it didn't believe it would happen and kept hoping it could be avoided. Otherwise, the world would have done everything—or much more than "everything"—not to allow this abyss. The war was unrealistic, absurd, and frankly unthinkable. And when you wake up in the midst of war, it remains the same: still unimaginable.

At the political level, the unimaginable was compounded by the fear of a huge phantom—a phantom that a corrupt and aggressive dictatorship had spent years constructing through propaganda. This phantom even managed to convince itself that it was powerful enough to capture Ukraine in just a few days with a blitzkrieg. It would be like a vacation for the soldiers—they would be greeted with flowers. A quick victory was guaranteed.

Fear tied our hands, and caution seemed the wisest option. Everyone waited until the catastrophe really began. Now, in Kyiv, and together with the whole world, I have to watch as houses, lives, and memories disappear in a huge fire.

And still, in the midst of war, in the midst of senseless death, injury, suffering, and loss, more crimes are predicted. Russia comes forward almost daily with old and new demands, always based on territorial claims. A new preface is being written into the war narrative once again. If its demands for more territories are rejected, Russia will announce even more war, even more death.

As I'm writing this entry, a friend calls to say that her mother, who still lives in Kharkiv, was out on the balcony when she spotted a man speaking Russian. He was relaying the coordinates for a bombing on the street outside her house. He was apparently a *navodchik*, an antiquated word meaning "gunner"—someone who decides the location of a strike and helps to shell peaceful districts. The distribution of food was supposed to happen next to her house. Perhaps that is why the *navodchik* chose this spot.

The father of another friend stayed in Kharkiv because the employees of his small company couldn't escape the city. He wanted to help people on the ground. For days he endured the rocket and mortar attacks unharmed. But now, in this city under fire, my friend is trying to find psychological help for her father. He can no longer understand where he is or what is happening around him.

In Kharkiv, during the first days of the war, the animals in a small private zoo were wounded. The zoo staff stayed in the city to care for them. Today, some of the staff were deliberately shot at on their way home from the zoo. Some were wounded. Some died.

An acquaintance of mine spent twelve days in her basement in a small town outside Kyiv—without light, almost without food. She was rescued today.

I myself was detained today on the street in Kyiv by an elderly couple. They noticed that I was taking photos and suspected that I might be spying for Russia. They took me to a checkpoint in the hope that I would be disarmed. And all I had wanted was to take a hopeful photo of the city. I wanted to show that food delivery services were running again, bringing meals to the elderly and the sick. The few remaining employees walk around the city to make deliveries! This means that those who need help but cannot shop for themselves will find a little more security and care.

Music

The windows in my little room are darkened with duvet covers. There's a light on, and it's reasonably comfortable. An app on my phone announces in a woman's voice, "The air raid is over." I'm experiencing one of those rare moments where I think I've discovered something fundamental, where I understand what photography is for. I've occupied myself with photography for a long time, but I've never understood it in practice as I do now.

Only with the help of photos can I remember the course of today's walk. In the daily life of war, only something like photography—unfamiliar, auxiliary, almost mechanical—is capable of holding together sequences and memories.

When I went for a walk, my thoughts were still on the morning news, and I hardly paid attention to the street. With a deep sadness, I had to admit to myself the very real possibility that we might eventually be forced to leave Kyiv. I'd known all along it might come to that, of course, but today the possibility really struck me again.

Then I thought, "At least I'm still in Kyiv for now. I must cherish every minute and look around—to see the city, the streets, the people." This was somewhat naive, however, and I quickly sank back into my thoughts, hardly noticing what was going on around me.

The soldiers of the Territorial Defense were warming their hands. I saw the beautiful faces of two young women who laughingly told me that they belonged to the "Volunteer Army of Ukraine." They gave me their phone numbers. What that meant was: maybe we will meet again.

To my surprise, a little later I heard music. I was walking through the sculpture park, along Landscape Alley. From a distance I heard drums, bells, and a melodic whistling. The music came from the hills. I listened very carefully. The sounds grew a little louder with every step. Then I spotted a small group of men and women playing musical instruments in the distance. What a combination of different fragments, tones, and pauses. I listened, enchanted. They finished and approached me, passing along with friendly glances. I was so impressed seeing these musicians and listening to their renditions that I can't remember what happened afterward.

But thanks to photographs, which I continue to try to take, another important scene comes to mind. The municipal workers of Kyiv were out in the city, using spray paint to cover up tourist maps of the city center that appear on signs all around that area. The workers were accompanied by armed members of the Territorial Defense. I was allowed to take photos as long as no faces could be recognized in the images.

Now my memory jumps to another musically related episode: on March 8, International Women's Day, I went to the pharmacy with my mother. On the way, we met an elderly woman carrying a rose. My mother approached her. They chatted and exchanged contact information so they could help each other in case of any emergency.

Then the woman began to recite a poem she had recently written in Russian. It was about dictatorship and war, and ended with a promise that this absolute senselessness, this evil, would never prevail. The woman looked modest in her headscarf, while the musical lines of her poem carried a distinct melody with their directness.

The signs with tourist maps were painted over so that saboteurs, who are constantly trying to enter Kyiv and other cities, will not be able to use them. Rumor has it that they often don't have smartphones and get lost in the streets.

Today's news was excruciating. I think of the songs the people here continue to sing. I think of the music.

The air raid warning sounds again. I wait and hope that the sky will soon be closed.

Saturday, March 12

Too Tired for the Shelter

It was a sleepless night. The air raid sirens sounding over the city kept me up all night. But I was too tired to go to the shelter. I heard explosions and hoped that no one was injured. Then I tried to find out what was going on, but on Telegram there were only reports about other places—the blockades that Russian units were establishing around cities; the residents of those cities who spend day and night in the nightmare of a siege.

My plan for the day was to pick up my bulletproof vest that had finally been delivered. Then I would visit a lady known to be a sort of concierge, watching over houses in the neighborhood and keeping an eye on things. There are many such concierges in the city, but since the beginning of the war this lady has taken on an additional task: she must make sure that nothing is stolen from the abandoned apartments. Her name has a comforting ring to it that reminds me of childhood—Dussia.

Tonight, like every other night, I was overcome with fear. The sirens, with their long and melancholy trumpet notes, made me uneasy. I imagined armed strangers invading Kyiv, bringing silence to every street and every house and every feature of this city, until everything vanishes. Again and again I told myself, "It's just a brief panic attack—it will be over soon."

When I called Dussia for the first time, I could sense both tenderness and restlessness in her voice. I told her that one of the residents from her building who had fled the city had asked me to check in on her, which she was happy to hear. Because she lives alone, with no one to help her with her duties, she can never be relieved of her watch. She also lives in the building, and is afraid to go out, even to shop for food. Dussia thought that I sounded suspicious at first, so she kept me on the phone a while to convince herself that she could trust me.

I visited her in her small concierge room on the first floor. There was only space for a table and a sofa. The TV was on. She said, "So many people are escaping Kyiv, but I have nowhere to go. My relatives live outside Chernihiv, and you know what happened there. Where should I go? Where can I go?"

In her face I saw helplessness, but she had made her decision to stay. Fifteen families remained in the large apartment block she looked after; they needed someone to rely on. I tried to lighten the mood with some not entirely clever jokes. I was happy that she smiled at me, and I decided to visit her again soon.

In the evening, a friend's message arrived. She wrote that a group of women and children had tried to escape on foot today from an occupied village outside Kyiv. The village retains a name from Soviet times: Peremoga ("Victory"). The group was fired on as they left the village. Seven women and one child died. My friend said she understands why Ukrainians use the word "genocide" when describing this war. I don't know if it is the right word to use. I read her message over and over again.

From time to time I look at the comments that readers post online about this diary, and I often see similar arguments. I recognize these sentences from analytical articles, where "experts," who for years played the role of opponents to the Russian regime, express their allegedly independent opinions that always happen to be the same:

The Russian regime is inhumane and murderous, but also very dangerous and unpredictable. We cannot imagine what this ghastly person will do to the world if he loses the war in Ukraine. If he wins, however, then the world will gain a little time to prepare and consider how to better understand the situation.

This kind of reasoning teaches the world that if one barely interferes, suffering will not spread too far. Fear continues to sell, with no sanctions imposed on it.

We are now living through the consequences of this thinking. Like all the great crimes of the world, it spreads through many languages in a thousand different voices. This isn't just a question of history and suffering repeating over and over again, but also of the habit of making sacrifices and satisfying monsters and perpetrators of violence.

And so this monster flexes his strength by attacking women and children who leave "Victory" on foot and cannot protect themselves against his heavy artillery.

Sunday, March 13

An Unexpected Gift

When dusk comes, I turn on as many lights as possible in the room in my apartment where I read. At this time of day, it's not yet dangerous to have the lights on. It's still somewhat bright outside, so the contrast with my windows isn't too extreme. This overexposure can only last for thirty or forty minutes—then evening comes with the necessity of spending it in near darkness.

Today, I want to write about two meetings. I went back to the street in Kyiv where I once lived for several years. With amazement I saw that welcoming lights were shining in a cozy cafe, which like most cafes in the city had been closed since the beginning of the war. I went inside and ordered a cappuccino—a drink I'm always on the lookout for since the war started and, if successful, which I enjoy in a new way each time.

It is a game I play with myself. Every day I wonder if a cafe will be open on my route. When I manage to find a cup, I'm immensely happy, as if I've received an unexpected gift.

The cafe was open because an employee who had quit before the war offered to return and work alone. This former employee's name is Aleksej. It was his birthday today, but he didn't celebrate. He said to me, "I wanted to do something, anything, so I thought it over and decided that the best thing to do was to open the cafe."

He has nowhere else to go, he said, because he fled Luhansk Oblast after the Donbas war in 2014. He doesn't want to leave Kyiv now. He keeps thinking about his parents and sister, whom he hasn't seen for years and who live somewhere near Luhansk, in the occupied territories.

When I asked about his birthday, Aleksej said, "Everything has lost its former meaning. I only remembered yesterday that today is my birthday. Besides, it's Sunday." I said that maybe tomorrow, Monday, there would be more visitors to the cafe. Then we both had to laugh because it no longer makes any difference whether it is Sunday, Monday, or Friday. Breaks in the rhythm of life arise differently during wartime and come without warning.

Then I met a couple with two small dogs. The woman's name was the same as mine, Yevgenia. They initially claimed to have escaped from Chernihiv, only to reveal later that they had not named their actual town out of caution. In reality, they had escaped from a village on the left bank of the Dnieper, in Kyiv Oblast.

They are both eighty-five years old, and along with four relatives, they are refugees. They're all staying in a small apartment in Kyiv that belongs to their grandchildren. They said that they used to think it was best for their children to have lives separate from their own, but now they live together because they couldn't imagine traveling any farther away from their village than Kyiv.

Although their dogs couldn't stand the rockets and explosions, the couple had remained home until the very last moment—and only then fled to Kyiv. The man looked at me. He asked, "Do you at least have a place to live here?" I nodded and barely managed to say "Yes."

Rockets over Kyiv

Today has been a day without end. The sirens won't stop howling. By now, the residents of Kyiv have gotten used to the fact that the city is comparatively safe, at least for the moment. Even people from outside the city have fled here. Families from Irpin, from Bucha, from Vorsel come to Kyiv. In some villages there has been no food or water since the beginning of the war.

Escape is risky. Some families and groups of refugees have to walk long distances to reach safety. In some areas that are perpetually under fire, electricity has been down since the second day of the war. I heard from some acquaintances that a couple with five children were due to reach Kyiv yesterday. They had been on the road for days, since February 25 to be exact, not drinking fresh water but thawing snow, unable to be reached by phone.

This morning I talked with Sophia about fear. Sophia is eighteen years old. She's a medical student who helps as a paramedic in the volunteer army. She is scared, she said, but still she is ready to go to war.

As we talked, the gunfire grew louder and more threatening, but next to Sophia I felt strangely safe—as if her military uniform were a guarantee that nothing would happen to us. Her father—a business-man from the central Ukrainian town of Kropyvnytski, where the airport was shelled the day before yesterday—had been sent to the front in 2014. For this family, war, or even the idea of war, didn't exist until eight years ago. But since 2014, both daughter and father have lived with the thought of needing to defend their country.

Sophia said this war was inevitable: "I've said it over and over again. Even four years ago I was sure we had to prepare for it." I agreed with her, thinking how wise that would have been then. But I had also long believed the opposite, convinced that such a war was impossible. As we talked, I forgot that Sophia would have been fourteen when she began to mentally prepare herself for war. Her father was always at the front, so she couldn't stop seeing the reality of war. As recently as last summer, she herself had been to the Donbas, to the heavily shelled Avdiivka, a town north of Donetsk. She was there with the Ukrainian Hospitallers Medical Battalion.

"I remember my father calling from Kyiv at that time. In a quiet voice he told me, 'Two more of our soldiers were killed in the Donbas yesterday, and another house was shelled.'" That was always on So-phia's mind. And yet, when I talked to her, I thought she was far away from the actual war. She laughed and joked around, her expression only turning serious again with the sound of gunfire and artillery.

"When I was in Avdiivka," she said, "it was relatively quiet. I was lucky, and I was able to learn a lot in the hospital. Only two of our sol-diers were injured when I was there. But then came darker times." She paused. "Wait a second! I can't hear the air defense. That means targets in Kyiv might have been hit!" We had to interrupt our conversation.

On the way back to my home, I read the news. A missile had hit a high-rise building. Seventy people were evacuated, ten injured. One person was killed. At about the same time, a bus carrying refugees from the eastern Ukrainian town of Izyum was shelled. No one knows if there are any survivors. This all happened in the morning hours, when representatives of the Ukrainian government were negotiating with Russia.

I think the attack on Kyiv was a signal, a sign that no one in Ukraine can go to sleep thinking that they are safe in their house or apartment. The rockets breach the walls of the houses like the skin of the body. The whole idea of a house, of shelter and protection, is called into question.

When I write about the attacks and the violence, I use the word "war," but it hardly describes the terror, the targeted murder of the defenseless. "War" does not cover the merciless attacks against homes and buses carrying refugees. Official internationally recognized figures say that 2,357 people have been killed in Mariupol, and in Kharkiv 600 residential houses have been destroyed.

I wrote this text before going to sleep. Today, at five o'clock in the morning, my house shook with a strong explosion. I woke up with the feeling of cold spreading in my stomach. From the window I checked to see that everything was fine with the neighboring buildings, including my parents' building. I thought about leaving—I should at least make a plan to leave Kyiv.

How can the world put an end to this crime? This is not just a war but a continuous terrorist attack. And it looks like these crimes that subjugate and colonize the Ukrainian people are meant not only to intimidate us, but also to terrify the whole world. Despair and fear help make this terror possible.

Tuesday, March 15

In War, One Thinks Almost Only of War

The people of Kyiv are returning. It is hard to believe, but it is so. "All the residents are back in our building," a friend reported. "At night there is a light in every window."

I notice it myself. The street where I live is full of young faces, even though houses not far away were shelled yesterday. A kiosk with coffee and cake is open and, in front of the window, a small line has formed.

Many people are walking their dogs through the city, as if such walks were becoming normal again. It is sunny and warm, the cold wind has subsided, and everyone is trying to savor their time before the curfew begins. Once again, a long lockdown has been announced for Kyiv and no one will be able to leave their homes except to go to a shelter.

I watched a video statement from a government advisor who

usually delivers good news. He said Ukraine is winning the war, by and large, simply because Russia's attempts to divide the country, attack civil society, and seize major cities have failed. The sanctions have had a strong effect, but he insisted we still need some time to win militarily. Until then, unfortunately, Russian missiles could still hit some residential buildings—an apparently intentional strategy, he said. Other experts apparently have expressed similar views elsewhere, giving shape to a new reality.

In Mariupol, according to media reports, a hospital was captured by a Russian task force. The doctors are currently unable to leave—they are locked in the basement along with 400 residents from neighboring houses, all brought there by Russian soldiers. Many buildings around the hospital have been destroyed, and fighting continues in the streets.

This casts a shadow on the news that I was so hoping for: today, 20,000 people from Mariupol are finally able to leave the city through a humanitarian corridor. This is what our relatives, friends, and loved ones have spent weeks waiting for as we shudder and watch the battle for Mariupol. Many people have now been freed from a place where life no longer seems possible. And yet there are still those who stay—some because they are trapped in occupied hospitals, others because of their families, or life's general obligations.

An acquaintance of mine, a Ukrainian art scholar, fled from Irpin to Kyiv and on to Vinnytsia in central Ukraine. From there, she has written in great detail on Facebook about her grandmother, who lives in a beautiful little house in Irpin with a well-tended flower garden. I assumed the grandmother had fled to Kyiv by now too, and I wanted to inquire about her well-being and ask if she needed any help. I learned that she had absolutely refused to leave her house in Irpin. She can't imagine living anywhere else. My acquaintance tries to call her several times a day, but the number remains unreachable.

Is the celebratory mood in Kyiv today related to the opening of humanitarian corridors? Or is it that many analysts have been expressing reassuring, almost hopeful thoughts about the outcome of the war?

The number of victims is already so high that it is difficult to comprehend. Again and again, I hear the thundering and crashing of Russian shells destroyed midflight by the air defense over Kyiv. In war, one thinks almost only of war. The concepts of big politics—abstract discussions about the "theater of war," about what belongs to "the West" and what to Russia and Ukraine—serve as mental refuges within the intolerability of war. One recovers in the space of analytical thought, a space where these lofty, immaterial questions are discussed, where the matter at hand is no longer actual human lives but states whose strategies are often described as manifestations of their national traits.

Before curfew, I wanted to see the subway station that had been shelled last night. I had to pass through checkpoints and take detours to get a glimpse of the wreckage. Shards of glass remained scattered in a shockingly large radius around the station. A roof had caved in, vinyl doors had been deformed by the blast wave, and hundreds of broken windows stared blackly into the street. A circle of silence had formed around this place, where several houses and dozens of smaller stores had been damaged in one fell swoop.

The ruins formed an eerie scene. I saw some women standing in front of the damaged buildings for several minutes, looking at the destroyed section of the street, as if they wanted to memorize every crack, every broken windowpane, forever.

Wednesday, March 16

Tactical Retreat

One does not speak to a ruin. One contemplates it, holds it in one's mind. It is war's silent witness in the middle of the city. Looking at a ruin gives the observer a certain distance from events.

What does this distance mean? It is in no way an emotional distance, but a detachment that gives strength and the feeling that you can control how close the war comes to you. As a giant trace of an inhuman force, a ruin devours everything human that makes up the street you're standing on.

I keep thinking about what it means to observe the consequences of the bombardment in the city. Kyiv looks like a construction site— one not for building but dismantling.

In front of the ruins yesterday—among shattered glass, deformed scraps of metal, and pieces of the roof—a woman approached me and introduced herself. She was an elderly lady who was looking for cigarettes. The kiosk where she had bought them every day was so badly damaged that all the glass of the windows and doors had been blown out. The salespeople themselves were no longer around. Packs of cigarettes sat unprotected in the shop window. The lady asked everyone where she could buy a pack nearby. I suggested she leave money in the shop window and take some cigarettes as a kind of self-service. Then I asked her why she decided to stay in Kyiv during these uncertain times.

She told me that her mother, who turned 100 three months ago, died this past week. In the war's early days, it was unthinkable that she and her husband would leave the city. Now she was simply here. Maybe she would stay. Her eyes were shining—she even looked a little happy.

She was a mathematician, a scientist who came to Kyiv from Murmansk as a child. She told me the tangled story of her family and how they were saved time and again from war, hunger, and Stalin's repressions. She spoke melodically and with a delicate touch, interspersing many witty remarks, as if the words of her narrative had bound themselves together beforehand and merely awaited a listener. Despite her age, there was something young about her face, and she moved quickly and gracefully among the stones and splinters. Our conversation didn't last long, but I keep thinking about it. Sometimes in war you have the feeling that you don't want to lose other people, even after fleeting encounters. And now that I've described that meeting, I feel I've done something to really hold on to it.

The air raid sirens are silent for the moment. We are safe. During the curfew, authorities recommend darkening the windows, turning on the lights as little as possible. The streets are empty; the houses look abandoned. It's a relief to think that at least these houses aren't in danger right now as they try with all their might to mask the lives of their inhabitants, to make their residents invisible.

Urban life makes a tactical retreat during lockdown, all the while hoping to return again tomorrow, when the street will be seen as a street rather than a source of danger.

Mariupol is undergoing something quite different. Around 1,000 people whose houses had been destroyed found refuge in the Drama Theater, a large building in the city center. In satellite images, you can see that next to the theater, the Russian word for "children" was written twice in chalk in capital letters. Perhaps this word was written on the ground at risk of death in the hope that it would provide protection from the bombs and shelling.

The word looks like a warning, a dialogue with someone who could never imagine attacking such a place. One of my mother's friends, who had worked as a theater director in Kyiv with Russian colleagues, still insists that Russia is attacking only military infrastructure. When my mother objects, "But the apartment buildings are damaged," he replies, "That was a mistake, and believe me, they will punish the responsible parties!"

When I read the word "children" in these photos, I can understand the belief that no one would commit such an atrocity, even when the war has already become so horrific.

Today the theater in Mariupol was bombed—there's discussion of a "high-performance bomb." What does that mean? It means that the building no longer exists. As I write this, because of the constant shelling, relief workers cannot approach the site to comb the rubble for survivors.

I am safe. The air raid sirens have fallen silent and theoretically I could even go to sleep. Tomorrow is the beginning of another day. New events will come, and tomorrow we will speak of them and contemplate them instead of the theater in Mariupol. I can't imagine it. The days of the war should not draw to a close just like any other days in a life. Someone has allowed this war to happen. The world has deliberated, doubted, and still allowed it. It may be too late, but the sky over Mariupol must be closed at once!

The next morning, I learn that rescue workers were able to reach the rubble of the theater after all. From the bunker beneath the building, survivors are climbing out.

Friday, March 18

The Picture of the Man with the Cat

Thursday passed quickly but I want to say something about it even though I couldn't write anything the whole day.

Another air raid warning just ended and I finally have time to concentrate. Something important did in fact happen yesterday. But as soon as I try to write about it, the air raid warning with its threatening howl begins again—so I have at least another twenty minutes, maybe even an hour, until I know if I am really in danger. I think I'll have time to finish writing another entry.

I find photos of burning houses in Kyiv on the internet. I save these pictures so as not to forget them, but then can't remember what day they are from: this morning, yesterday, or the day before yesterday.

It occurs to me that this morning I saw a photo of a man with old professor's glasses standing in front of a multistory house. He wore a jacket that looked a little too big for him, and his face had a puzzled expression without appearing sad. With a desperate gesture, he pressed a beautiful long-haired cat to his chest. The cat clung to him with a shocked expression on its face. Its nose was injured and bleeding. The man had saved the cat—they had both survived.

A resident of a high-rise building in Podil died in an attack. Nineteen were injured, including four children. All this happened early in the morning. The man with professor's glasses lost his home. He ran out of the burning apartment with his cat and no bag, nothing else.

I recall the couple I had met in the neighborhood a few days ago, the older people with the two small dogs. They were both eighty-five years old and said, "We left our house as you see us now—without possessions. There was nothing we could take with us."

Different scenes from Telegram channels race through my head. I wish I could concentrate, but instead a number pops into my head: 222. That's how many people are said to have died in Kyiv since the war began. Four children among them. Many more have been injured. I can't do anything with this number. It is new and surprising. It includes not only civilians but also members of the Territorial Defense in our city.

Yesterday was the second day of the Jewish holiday Purim. I went to Podil to pick something up from the post office, and I decided on my way back that I would visit the synagogue where my friends were celebrating.

To reach this old Kyiv district I walked down Andriyivskyy Descent, a tourist street where the writer and satirist Mikhail Bulgakov once lived and his museum now stands. The Descent—normally one of the most crowded streets in Kyiv—was absolutely deserted at noon. In the midst of this desolation, I noticed that two cafes were open. I entered one of them, ordered an espresso, and learned that the owners were giving out free coffee to everyone. They wanted to reopen the cafe "so that the people of Kyiv could feel that peace is on its way back and will soon return fully and irrevocably," as one employee explained.

There was a line in front of the post office. My package, an order of various device chargers, had not arrived. I looked around with the vague desire to buy something. There were a couple of options, but there wasn't much to grab my attention. The air raid warning started blaring. I wanted to stay a little longer with the other people in the shop. I noticed that I wasn't the only one ambling from shelf to shelf with searching, disappointed glances. It was more pleasant to stay together in this small space than to walk home alone through the bare and sunny streets.

I forced myself to leave the shop and made my way to the synagogue. Once there, I found a small group of revelers in a prayer room in the back. They were following the commandment that one must be so drunk on this day that one can hardly tell a sinner from a saint. One member of the congregation is visually impaired and his friend accompanied him to the synagogue every day so that he could participate in prayer. My good friend, an artist, joined in the celebration. Everyone embraced several times. One individual even tried to raise a ruckus, but it was only in play.

My way home took me along the Andriyivskyy Descent again, since all other paths seemed unsafe.

On the way back I had the idea of photographing the most unspeakably banal views of Kyiv, replicating the photos that tourists always take when visiting the city for the first time. With this idea in mind I walked to the sculpture park. A few parents and their children were walking among the dog owners with their pets. I was going to take a photo of the scenery when I suddenly noticed purple-gray smoke drifting across the sky.

I hadn't heard the impact! Was it just a cloud? But then other people came up to me with worried faces and said, "Did you see that? It was a rocket! Where did it fall? Was anyone injured, or were any houses hit? Let's check the news!" But the news provided nothing. For several days now the media hasn't reported the damage immediately after a shelling, in case the aggressor corrects his targets and fires again.

Angry and terrified, I stood there watching the smoke. I felt something else that I can barely describe: What was happening in front of my eyes at that moment was a crime. The fire was so strong that the cloud of smoke continued to expand. I wanted to do something about this crime, though I couldn't figure out what to do. Still, I knew action was necessary, everything else could wait.

Nearby, parents called for their children and quickly left. I went home as well, wanting to write a diary entry, but felt a great exhaustion that I couldn't fight. I fell asleep without having written a word.

Deceptive Illusion

Today an old couple made their way through the wreckage on Sicho-vykh Striltsiv Street. They walked shakily past shards of broken glass and heaps of rubble.

The man, speaking to his wife, reproached an invisible enemy: "Look how many windows, how much glass has been smashed! Jesus. They haven't thought about the fact that they'll have to clean this up. All this chaos just to say, 'The Russians did this to us!'" The woman nodded and sighed to the rhythm of his criticism in all its desperation and sadness. They walked straight past me. I didn't approach them—their whole world was in a state of ruin.

This elderly pair, who have lived their lives surrounded by undying declarations of love between Russians and Ukrainians, two peoples bonded like brothers, didn't want to believe that fratricide was in full swing. Apparently they thought Ukraine was just staging the destruction, and that the war would spare each nation's true love for the other, like untouched nature.

On the ground, pigeons pecked at breadcrumbs among the pieces of glass. Despite the damage to this radically altered landscape, a woman had come to the marketplace, as she does every day, to feed the birds. It was sunny and disturbingly quiet. One feels free on these streets, as if a dangerous illusion beckons you to take a long walk, as if that would be safe. Lately, no two hours pass without the sirens howling; but today nothing has sounded since 1:00 p.m..

Caution and fear remain in the air. People discuss the safest spots in their apartments—where to sleep and where, under any circumstances, not to sleep. These thoughts infect my own. I've been sleeping in my small study until the sirens start wailing between four and five in the morning, at which point I move to the hallway, where I spread blankets out on the floor. I try to fall asleep again on this colder and harder surface, a poor substitute for a mattress. The shelter where I spent the first nights of the war is overcrowded. One can hardly find a spot.

I was already asleep in the hallway when my mother woke me. "Something is burning. Can't you smell it?" she asked in the low voice she reserves for real danger.

I approached the window with an uneasy feeling and saw white smoke drifting down the street. An acrid smell came through the window. The news was silent. The curfew was still in place and both of us, my mother and I, decided to go back to sleep. Half awake, I thought how good it was to be in the corridor, protected. Then I woke to the first report: a garbage dump outside Kyiv was burning and the wind was carrying the smoke into the city; a village had been attacked too—Novi Petrivtsi—but without apparent success for the aggressors.

Nobody was murdered; nobody died as a result of this smoke! So perhaps this mini-ecological crisis was a stroke of luck. Maybe the invaders had wanted to fire on residential buildings but hit a pile of garbage instead.

Most of the shelling takes place in the morning between four and six. Upon waking again, Kyiv could almost be characterized as calm, lacking any urgent concern. And yet anxiety grows with each day of war. Danger lies behind anything that used to be just a minor breach of normality not worthy of a second thought—air filled with dust or smoke, a loud knock in the distance. Even a day without disturbance cannot be trusted. One assumes the break in attacks is preparation for something worse.

At sunset, during the last rays of light, I met up with Lisa, a designer, not far from my house. She told me that she feels safe in Kyiv at the moment. A flower store was giving away bouquets. She carried two bouquets with her, planning to give one away as a gift. She pulled up a video on her phone to show me her town, Ochtyrka in northeastern Ukraine. The town has been in the news nonstop, and her father, a member of the Territorial Defense, is still there. At the start of the war, Lisa feared for his life and couldn't sleep, but now that Ochtyrka has been almost entirely destroyed, she told me she is strangely confident he will be fine. He has been saved repeatedly by coincidences and miracles.

All I saw in the video was scorched earth, burnt walls, and piles of black metal. "This was the center of our city," Lisa explained in a calm voice. "This was our municipal administration building, this was the arts and culture center, and here was the school I attended."

Sunday, March 20

Drones over Kyiv

I am trying to write, but I can't start. The air raid warning has been blaring for two hours. It is then echoed by the sirens that signal an ongoing attack, as if within one warning a second is waiting.

On Telegram I see the headline "KYIV IS BURNING!" The accompanying videos show rows of blazing houses—not just a single house, but an entire apartment block on fire.

Ten minutes ago I heard a loud explosion. I had just been thinking that I should finally sit down to write, but after the explosion I called my parents and friends to make sure they were safe.

An hour ago my mother called me to report that she had been watching the sky when a plane started firing at targets. We all heard gunfire—it was unclear where it was coming from. Then I read some reassuring news: enemy drones had been successfully eliminated. But almost immediately after that I looked out the window and saw two drones flying over my apartment. One stopped above the building that houses the local shelter. The drones flew high in the sky. It looked like they were being shot at.

My headache from the previous sleepless night disappeared. I felt cold, fearful, and determined—though I asked myself, "For what?" I called the police to pass on the coordinates of the drones. Then my parents and I briefly discussed whether it would be safer for us to go downstairs to the ground floors of our buildings. I decided to stay in my apartment and my parents decided to stay in theirs.

All the windows are dark and the lights are off; the same with the rest of the apartments I can see when I peek out my window. You try to make yourself invisible, to hide your house and sink into the darkness of the night, so as not to become a target. Strange images come to mind: being on the top floor of my apartment building I feel like I'm standing atop a flower with a long, thin stem. I can understand the fear and anger an insect might feel when accidentally knocked from a flower's petals.

In the meantime, high-definition videos of the attacks are being released. You can see the night being ripped apart by white flashes that grow taller than any skyscraper and blanket the houses below. When I try to tell myself that all this is happening right now to the people in my city—to those I meet every day on the streets, to passersby, doctors, vendors, artists, teachers—and that this deadly light threatens me at night too, I feel nausea and dizziness.

I can't close my eyes, can't find peace. That's what I want to describe to you. Tomorrow morning I will read this text again. If I do, it will mean that we survived the night.

I was outside for only a short time today. I said goodbye to a friend, an artist, who is leaving Kyiv tomorrow. Then I met a second friend, also an artist, who returned to Kyiv to join the Territorial Defense as a paramedic.

An acquaintance sent me a letter from Melitopol, which is occupied by the Russian army. A friend of his is searching for escape routes. This friend, his wife, and their child are hiding in a small apartment, slowly running out of food. The Russian secret service and military are arresting residents who continue to demonstrate against the occupation. Demonstrators are shot in the legs. Nobody can find a way to help Melitopol now. There is no escape, and people are being kidnapped.

A friend today used the word "genocide" to describe our current situation. This word penetrated deep into my mind. I still have a hard time adopting it. The term is the wrong size. As with other words of its kind, it is both a little too small and much too big, like borrowing someone else's clothing. Still—and this surprises me—it does in part describe the situation of Ukraine.

The apartments in Kyiv look peaceful, even during war. Neighborhood balconies are blanketed in colorful sheets, which are supposed to conceal and protect residents. This is the sort of photograph I wanted to choose for today's entry, even though it might not be the most fitting: the sheets look nice and innocent, and say little about death.

Is it possible to condemn me, my city, the people of Mariupol, the people of Melitopol and of all those other cities to death? Is it possible to play this game of annihilation with us, in front of the whole world? I keep thinking about these questions. What happened to us all that this became possible?

I think the answer will determine the future of a great many people. My cousin, a singer who is now in Kyiv, sings a lullaby for me. The burden of these past twenty-five days has been more than enough to bear. This war is destroying everything that has been achieved since the nightmare of the Second World War. Putin and his unlawful armies must be stopped.

Monday, March 21

"Kyiv will be as clean as Berlin!"

A man was staring at me, pale with stress. He was an elderly gentle-
man holding a large, hand-tied broom, and he stood next to three
big bags of trash from the street. He was a neighborhood building
manager I hadn't yet met. He noticed that I wanted to take his picture.
After a while he approached and asked me if I was "working for the
enemy." I showed him my passport and my press credentials and asked
him why he stayed in Kyiv. Satisfied with my documents, he leaned
forward, his face growing large, as in a close-up. Then he spoke to me
confidentially, though in the tone of an official announcement: "I am
proud to be here in Kyiv during these difficult days, taking care of the
cleanliness of our city!" He added, "Kyiv will be as clean as Berlin, just
as clean! We will achieve it."

He told me that he had lived outside of Berlin for a while, in

Bernau: "A very nice little town that has seen so much history. It was even part of the GDR. Wonderful people!" I grew curious. Every day I see people taking care of Kyiv, whether cleaning up or working on repairs. Next to all the bullet-ridden doors and shattered windows, I see people using plywood to cover and preserve this heap of broken shells we call a city, so that one day we can install real glass panes, doors, and shop windows again.

The building manager wanted to say more about Berlin and Bernau—about the generosity of the people there and how much they would do for others—but just then two members of the Territorial Defense approached us. They asked me to show my passport and credentials again. They looked anxiously at my camera and asked me several times to be careful when I publish pictures.

Yesterday's terrifying shelling was apparently the result of a Tik-Tok video that had revealed the location of Ukrainian tanks. The tanks, briefly visible in the background of the video, were long gone at the time of the bombing. But the aggressor sought to strike these tanks and, as a result, reduced a huge apartment building and a large shopping mall to burnt, black skeletons. The apartments in the building, with their small, private, hidden worlds, no longer exist. People were injured and some lost their lives. The number of lives lost always changes. One must count the casualties again and again.

Photographs can be dangerous. They can reveal things without intending to. They transform the city into a target just by existing, even though the documentation of one's life through pictures has become a modern habit that can help us process pain, fear, and danger. While words can be deceptive, a photograph seems to capture something irrevocably while at the same time it speaks for itself. One wants to give an account, not with words, but with something irrefutable like an image.

Today I wanted to write my diary entry earlier than usual. I no longer wanted to join sentences together while shivering in the corridor when it's dark outside, when it's so late that Russia decides: "Now is the time to shell residential buildings again." Analysts claim that the attacks are taking place deep in the night because of the expectation that Ukrainian air defenses will not be as sharp then, due to exhaustion. A long lockdown has been announced for tomorrow. People will not be allowed to leave their homes. Despite the impending curfew, there were a few people out in the streets today.

I went to the train station with my mother to see if we could get tickets for ourselves and our relatives. As we walked through the old city, I recalled how my mother had once shown me around the area, as if she were reading a story to a child. The train station wasn't as crowded as we had expected. All the shops had closed, and the only tickets available were for the evacuation trains. Several of these tickets were standing room only, and because some of my relatives have health issues that prevent them from standing for too long, we decided to look for tickets again later.

At the station I saw a young woman with a baby. She asked me if I knew whether there was a train to Chernivtsi, in the south, not far from the Romanian border. She was from a village outside Kyiv and hoped to find safety in Chernivtsi. She smiled, and then her face turned grave: "But my mother is still in our village. She didn't want to leave! I want to go back! I want to go home!"

My mother and I walked back down the street and tried to cheer each other up with a few jokes. Then we saw little yellow buses with red crosses heading toward us, in the direction of the train station. On each bus was written "Irpin," a place north of Kyiv where many artists and writers once lived and where now people die every day. Russia is annihilating this small town block by block. In the dusty bus windows, we saw the gray, tired faces of old people and children, all staring somewhere far away, into the distance. We stopped and looked. I couldn't take a photo.

In the evening I saw that train tickets were being sold again. Without pausing to consider, I bought six tickets for Friday. My parents still don't want to leave Kyiv. I really don't know what we should do. But there should be enough time before Friday to decide. After all, what is happening cannot last that long. This war can and should be interrupted at last. It must stop.

The Houses That Disappeared

A day in lockdown, without being allowed to leave the house, alone with the news and conjectures about the future. The end of the war is continually announced like a weather forecast. Some experts express themselves in newspapers, others through long and reassuring video monologues. In this way, by leaping into a distant news stream, one can slowly accept what is happening to my country. At the same time, such thoughts are unbearable. I push them away. Besides, I know that "my country" sounds abstract enough as an idea that one could "accept" what is happening—but you can never understand how something so brutal can be done to people.

When I walk through Kyiv, I see men and women standing like little statues, looking at their phones. They don't seem to want to know what's happening in their immediate surroundings anymore.

They read the news because only there, it seems, the secret answers to the dark questions that arise every day in new and uncertain ways are hidden. Many phone numbers have been disconnected. A humanitarian catastrophe is unfolding in all occupied territories. Hunger reigns, people are kidnapped and arrested.

Perhaps the tight narratives of the news cycle only testify to something that is missing. What's really missing right now are words. I'm in my apartment and have found some time to write—but I can barely develop a thought.

I watch video clips of the shelling on my phone. They are shared on Telegram channels, posted by residents of Kyiv. I see how silver streaks glow and then settle from the sky onto the rooftops. Some claim it's phosphorus ammunition; others think it's rocket fire from a Grad system. A few of the districts of Kyiv, including mine, were shelled today.

Then I think for the first time that this footage could be a forgery, that it's a recording of another reality. It's not about Kyiv at all. Is it possible that right now—as I write this in my apartment while most of my neighbors spend the night in shelters—Grad missiles are flying through the air and white phosphorus is raining down on someone's home, not so far from here, in my own city?

I miss all the walls, all the houses of this city that I still haven't seen, that I never photographed, that have already been destroyed, now unrecognizable, a pile of ashes.

Around noon today a powerful strike could be felt throughout my house. The rules of news coverage are changing, so it's not clear right away what attacks are happening where. Only the body of the house and one's own body sense the danger. For now, they have become the most immediate sources of information.

A few hours ago, I spoke on the phone with Elena, an employee at a zoo outside Kharkiv, an area subject to constant onslaught. She is the director of the zoo's children's theater, where children perform together with dogs, mice, and rats. Since the war started, employees have been trying to feed and evacuate the animals. But as soon as the Russian army sees any cars, bullets begin to fly.

On March 7, Elena tried to reach the zoo one last time in order to bring food to the animals. On the phone she explained to me that many animals remain in their pens: "The deer were shot at. Some of them died. Others managed to escape through the ruined fence into the forest. When we arrived by bus, the shelling started. We ran out of the bus with the feed and made it to the pens. Some great apes had been shot. We ran through the damaged rooms trying to distribute as much of the feed as possible. Then we ran to the bus, but the driver was already dead. We tried to get another car to go back and transport his body to the city. Another colleague was fatally injured. Only one other person and I were able to escape."

"I can't cry," she went on to say. "I can't even believe what happened. I keep seeing the exhibit window where the monkeys were waiting for us. Many of them were standing there with babies pressed against their bodies. They were hoping for food, but we didn't manage to feed them that day." Elena has stopped going to the zoo for the moment, but other staff members are trying to reach the pens so that the animals, the ones still alive, don't die of hunger.

I don't want to write a "last" sentence. Every day we encounter our choices.

"Risk of injury!"

It was a day of contradictions, as if different realities were fighting one another. I woke up and saw white smoke outside. The air itself smelled burnt. The air raid warning was sounding, in addition to a command: "Do not approach your windows! There is a risk of injury!"

But a few hours later, around noon, the air became clean again. I had to do some shopping and was eager to leave the house after a long lockdown. But when I finally left my apartment, the sirens began to howl once more. I wanted to hurry home, but then I spotted two young people on a bench, in the middle of a peaceful conversation, as if the air raid warning had never sounded.

They were two students, Nikolaj and Sonia. Sonia explained that she was studying law and had remained in Kyiv almost by accident. Twice she had planned to leave, but each time her departure had fallen through for different reasons. Now they both try not to stray far from their neighboring apartments and try to study on their own when they have time. They don't want to be taught—they say it's unimaginable under these circumstances. Teaching is an organized transmission of knowledge, work structured by others. That no longer makes sense. Nevertheless, they think that knowledge will continue to exist and remain important, so it seems reasonable to go on learning autonomously.

Together we tried to formulate this thought more clearly, but we didn't quite succeed. They said that on April 4, depending on the circumstances, their formal education will begin again.

We talked about the air raid warnings that go off several times a day and always portend new dangers and new attacks. With every siren you hope nobody will be injured. They both said that they didn't hear the last warning—that's why they were sitting in the park, talking and trying to enjoy this sunny day despite the fatigue of many sleepless nights.

Out in the streets, I saw young women and men jogging through the shriek of sirens, on this first warm day of the year. Two florists had opened unexpectedly—I met a couple of pedestrians with bouquets in their hands. A woman who had just bought flowers was passing a recently reopened cafe on her way home after work. She stopped next to me and, in the middle of the street, we both read the news on her phone.

I wanted to tell her how brave she was for staying and working in Kyiv. But she interrupted me and said that the really brave people are those who are gathering in the occupied cities of Kherson and Berdyansk to protest against the occupiers. People disappear there all the time: some are arrested and deported to Russia, while others are shot at and injured during the protests.

She told me she has family near Berdyansk, in the small town of Polohy, which is also occupied by the Russian army. She often loses her lines of contact with Polohy. The internet connection there is unstable, the power goes out, food is scarce. Her relatives are able to survive mainly because a small bakery in the neighboring village supplies the whole district with bread. "Logistics can fail," the woman said. "Food warehouses can be blocked off. Yet sometimes there are people who keep things running despite everything. At the moment, this bakery is saving lives."

I was reminded of the news stories I keep reading about Russia attacking warehouses where provisions are stored. There are repeated attempts to cut off Kyiv from food supplies as well. The same thing is happening in Chernihiv, one of the most beautiful cities in Ukraine: it has been continuously shelled and there is hardly any water to be found, in addition to the lack of electricity and heating.

I know an elderly woman who recently traveled to Chernihiv because she lived alone in Kyiv and wanted to escape her loneliness. In vain I tried to reach her by phone. Chernihiv is in such great danger that the bodies of those who died in the attacks lie in the streets—for days they cannot be transported and buried on account of the continuous artillery fire.

There were few pedestrians on the streets in my neighborhood today, but the ones I did see were spreading warmth. Time and again I watched people hug each other. Even in the grocery store, surrounded by hurried customers, a man and woman stopped to hug. I probably stared at the scene a bit too long. At one point, the woman turned to me and said in an almost cheerful voice, "I haven't seen him in two weeks. He's back from the war, and he's alive!"

Thursday, March 24

The Smell of Burning Forests

A little girl looked at me with a friendly expression. She was coloring the backrest of a wooden bench with a piece of chalk. She tried to tell me something, but she was interrupted by her grandfather, who seemed annoyed. "Listen here," he said to me in a somewhat brazen voice, "I told my daughter, 'Let's buy that apartment in Kyiv.' But she replied, 'Nobody wants to live in Kyiv, with its stuffy big-city air! We should get a nice apartment under the green trees of Bucha, outside of Kyiv.' And, being the foolish person I am, I agreed!" He looked at me reproachfully, as if I were the one who had persuaded him to buy an apartment in a pleasant suburb now smothered in fire, rockets, and mortar shells.

I didn't even want to talk to him at first, but he had called out to me and asked me to walk a few steps in his direction. It was already evening, almost curfew. The little park I passed was deserted, but it left an impression of being on guard.

The air raid warning had just finished. I thought I had a few minutes for a little conversation before I needed to head for the shelter. When he mentioned Bucha, I instantly decided to spend as much time with them as they wanted. The girl, who was about six years old, told me in a serious voice, "For two weeks we lived in the basement! Twenty-one adults and seven children."

The grandfather still seemed angry with me. "I come from a city where most people speak Russian. I come from Dnipro. But part of our family lives in Bucha and here in Kyiv. Two weeks in the basement with only water, some food, almost no heating, and barely any electricity! Constant shelling, especially when we tried to sneak a little fresh air. And then they found us! The Russians came to us in the cellar and explained—no, they barked—that they had come to denazify us. 'If I were not seventy years old,' I answered them, 'I would rather throw you out than talk to you! Don't speak to me, not even for a second!' Now I'm here with my granddaughter. They tried to force us to leave the basement…."

He continued to recount what happened, but the story unraveled. At the end he got so furious that he said to me, "You should go there. To Bucha! If you were there, you wouldn't look at me like that, you would understand everything. And here, in Kyiv, nothing is apparent yet!"

It's evening now, and I'm sitting in my room. The air is slowly filling with the faint smell of something burning. Somewhere far away, on the right bank of the Dnieper, the forests are in flames after fierce rocket fire. Two large apartment blocks are reported to have been hit. The number of victims is not yet known.

Today, a childhood friend lost his family home. A week and a half ago, he left it in a hurry and with great difficulty, along with his uncle, who resisted, not wanting to leave under any circumstances. When I was younger, I used to visit his house all the time. I try to remember the rooms. I recall the traditional living room of a small house with a low ceiling, a resplendent wooden cabinet with old photographs on the shelf behind a glass panel, and the meals my friend's grandmother used to prepare for us. This memory isn't accompanied by any feeling at all, or so it seems.

Perhaps it will rain during the night, and the smoke will disappear, hopefully quickly. You have to drink a lot of water right now. That's what they recommend on the Telegram channels where people share pictures of the fires.

A downtrodden salesman who lives in my building reminded me that the war started exactly a month ago, on February 24. We both decided not to dwell on such dates anymore. The little girl I met, along with her grandfather, would have had much more to say, I presume. It's good to fall asleep knowing that they were rescued, that they called me over and told me their story, ultimately asking where they could buy jeans in Kyiv. They hadn't brought a change of clothes with them when they left Bucha. In Kyiv, stores are slowly beginning to open again. The little girl and her grandfather will certainly be able to buy something soon.

Here in Kyiv

Today's goal: bring the train tickets I bought for my family and relatives back to the station so that someone else can use them. Online returns aren't working right now.

Early in the day: a short and somewhat ironic conversation with a child psychologist, Irina, who lives in Hirske, not far from Lysychansk and Rubizhne, towns under heavy artillery and rocket fire. The news reported that the day before yesterday phosphorus bombs were employed in Rubizhne, this small town in Luhansk Oblast that journalists would typically never visit. Nevertheless, Irina remains on-site because every day she provides support to schoolchildren, other kids, and elderly people. Our conversation was interrupted when I had to go to the train station and Irina had to pick up medicine delivered to her from another city. Pharmacies are no longer open in Hirske, and not a single ATM there works. Tomorrow we will continue our conversation.

As I was listening to Irina, I thought that it must be spine-chilling to remain in such a place. It was even harder to imagine how children, women, and elderly people continue living there. Irina said that the school where she worked as a psychologist and art teacher was shelled by rockets this morning.

Maybe friends of mine who live outside of Ukraine have a similar difficulty imagining why we are still in Kyiv. What does it mean, really, to expose yourself to danger, even if only relative danger? From the outside, if viewed unkindly, it might even seem like a position that exudes ambiguity or indecision.

Russia exploited this ambiguity in 2014 to portray the people who chose not to flee the occupied territories of the Donbas as pro-Russian. Danger and inaccessibility functioned like a barrier at the time, so the media would report anything—probable or improbable—about the region.

My family wants to leave Kyiv; we had already planned our exit. But as the day of departure ruthlessly approached, they had more and more complaints and objections.

Here in Kyiv, where every day you come across friends, acquaintances, and strangers you end up helping, you manage somehow to bear the unbearable news and events. The daily restlessness and the incessant air raid sirens structure your time, merging powerfully with the flow of your consciousness, which might otherwise choose to linger on a painful thought as a passenger lingers at a bus stop.

My mother said to me today that she has not cried since the war began, but that my father almost cried when he learned that on March 20 in the small town of Kreminna—also in Luhansk Oblast, a little north of Hirske—a retirement home was shot to pieces by a tank. Almost all fifty-six residents were killed.

I listened to my mother and realized I somehow missed this inconceivable event. I felt ill. Then I felt anger rising within me and I too wanted to cry. At the same time, I couldn't really grasp the incident. I pictured my father's face as he read that news, and only through this image could I sense something burning and bleak.

We decided to postpone our departure for a few days, and perhaps to prepare a little better this time. And we resolved to return to Kyiv as soon as possible.

On the way back from the train station, my mother and I met two people from the military who were sitting in front of a grocery store drinking coffee. They showed us a picture of a boy, only fourteen years old, posing in a uniform next to some soldiers.

"We are going to our military positions today to fetch him," one of the soldiers explained. "He followed his father and wants to fight shoulder to shoulder with him, but he is too young. They have clearly lost everything—their house, their family—and now all he wants is to fight. We understand, of course, but cannot allow it." They were obviously proud, of both their mission and also of the boy's determination. They smiled with a little bit of tenderness, and their good mood even managed to infect us.

A Gap in the Window

This evening I couldn't close the kitchen window. Some hidden metal piece had broken, and the window would not completely close. A gap remained, you could hear the wind blowing outside, and I feared that if there were another fire in the area, my apartment would fill with smoke. It was already evening, and I was darkening the windows. To do this I always gather thick duvet covers—with such friendly and familiar blankets hanging over the windows, my kitchen becomes a safe place where I can spend the evening. With the windows darkened and the light outside almost extinguished, air still penetrated through the gap. I decided to call my neighbor Andrij, a doctor, to ask him for help. But he was in a bomb shelter, where he spends almost every night offering medical assistance. Our phone conversation calmed me down somewhat, although it was a bit absurd.

"Don't worry about it," he said. "The oil repositories aren't burning anymore and it's going to rain. Thanks to the gap, you are going to finally get some fresh air at night!"

"When do you think this will come to an end?" I asked. This has become a typical rhetorical question.

"It's becoming quite clear that soon they won't be able to do anything. We'll drive them out."

"I heard Boyarka was shelled. How is your mother?" His mother lives in that village, just outside of Kyiv.

"Part of a missile hit close to her house. But she's doing fine." In the photos I could find of that area, the aftermath of this attack looked like someone had bitten off a piece of a wall as if it were an apple, or a nightmarish illustration of the gingerbread house in "Hansel and Gretel."

"Can you imagine them running around Boyarka in small groups, firing at the commuter trains?" he asked. "That's what the saboteur groups are busy with now."

"But that's not in the news at all," I remarked.

"They just haven't written about it yet. My relatives there told me about it."

Other relatives of Andrij live in the occupied villages near Chernihiv. His relatives tell him that Russian soldiers raid homes and stores in search of alcohol. You can see them in the streets, often quite drunk. They gather to fire at apartment buildings and buses. They shell the trains that connect small towns. They keep breaking into the apartments and houses of the villagers, who, in talking to the soldiers, realize how little the occupiers know about the actual progress of the war. The soldiers' smartphones have been taken away from them. Russian military officials claim that Kyiv is already half occupied and that Odessa has been under Russian control for a long time, along with many other such successes. The soldiers ask about villages and use outdated national maps from 2015, when many places had different names. Eventually the soldiers try to take the cell phones of Andrij's relatives and other villagers. They do this to sever peoples' connections to the outside world, and perhaps to acquire some information themselves.

Andrij sounded chipper and sardonic. Despite everything that's happening, his relatives keep calling him and reporting on all that's going on in their village.

I forgot about the window. I remembered it only when I heard the air raid sirens during the night, with the stormy wind carrying the sound of distant explosions into my apartment.

I thought I had taken a lot of pictures today, but when I looked at the files, I realized how few there were. I was in one of the largest underpasses in Kyiv—in the city center, on Khreshchatyk Street, where I spent a large part of my childhood. All exits were monitored, and the underpass, typically crowded with little shops and hurried pedestrians, was empty, storing the sounds of war like a shell stores the sound of the sea. With trembling hands, I began to film part of the underpass. I thought that such a small video could say a lot about what was happening in the country. I counted every second as I filmed, afraid that someone would misunderstand my reasons for recording.

I wanted to write more today about Irina, an acquaintance from the small eastern town of Hirske whom I spoke to on the phone yesterday. But I can't find the words. The mother of her son's wife, an elderly retired woman, lives in Mariupol, across the street from the Drama Theater. She collects old porcelain, jewelry, and trinkets.

The mother's daughter, Irina's daughter-in-law, works as a doctor in the maternity ward of the hospital that was shelled—the shelling that made headlines around the world. One of her pregnant patients died. A few days after the shelling, bombs hit the cellar where her mother was hiding. Almost everyone in that cellar was killed, including her mother. Her father survived, but he won't leave Mariupol until he buries his wife. The shelling is so heavy, though, that a funeral isn't possible. Almost nothing remains of a woman's love for porcelain, or her memories. Only a story that is impossible to tell.

What is happening in Ukraine right now, what we are all experiencing, will define our existence forever. But not only ours. One must find the courage to stop the aggressor. The world will never forgive itself for these crimes.

Endless Cannonades

My previous entry was an eternity ago. At least that's how I perceive it. I may have missed only one day, but it feels like my German has slipped away and I'm no longer able to express my thoughts in this language. When I stop to reflect, Russian, Ukrainian, and English mingle to form the voice in my head.

Time sometimes runs too fast—days and hours seem to differ rapidly from one another. A feeling of security arises under the ongoing bombardment, and becomes unbearable: it seems to be cobbled together from counterfeit sensations.

An artist, the acquaintance of a good friend, lives on the outskirts of Kyiv. She says that the shelling sounds much louder in the forest than it does near me, in the center of town—as if there is fighting among the trees, someone on the hunt, shooting at someone else. Reflecting on the audible messages of gunfire coming from all around her, she wondered: What if she lay down on a forest path and decided to accept her own death? She thinks this could be somewhat liberating.

Tomorrow, talks between Ukrainian and Russian negotiators will take place in Istanbul. Perhaps that's why Kyiv has been shelled all day long. Early in the morning I heard endless cannonades, a composition of gunshots. My mother came by my apartment, and we went for a walk. We told each other funny stories and imagined that all the explosions were caused by our air defenses protecting the city. But then we heard a long, deep, rolling roar. A white line appeared, like the trace of an airplane, but short and uneven. It was the trail of a missile. We heard the explosion.

The news was silent even an hour after impact. For several days, reports of attacks and strikes have become increasingly delayed—so as not to give the enemy any hint about whether they have injured us. As a consequence, you hardly know where you are anymore. Where and when does the feeling of security—even if fleeting—begin, and where does it end? There remain only the messages on Telegram channels: "Many Kyiv residents are reporting explosions. But we don't want to write anything more specific about it now."

You can learn more from talk around town. At the kiosk where you can get one of the best espressos in Kyiv (or anywhere), the young barista confided in me that high-rises had been damaged within a fifteen-minute walk of his house. He reported this with a touch of irony in his intonation, as if he were talking about bad weather.

A good friend and human rights activist is now in Chernivtsi, in southwestern Ukraine. Her boyfriend, who fled Mariupol on foot, just arrived there. The residents of Mariupol are constantly trying to leave the city—without cars, and packing only the bare necessities. They flee in the direction of Berdyansk, where they then get picked up. Often news arrives that these pedestrians have been shot on the way. I can't imagine how people can learn about such crimes and not at once do something to stop them. A collective psychosis is sweeping Russian media right now, combined with an obvious enjoyment of impunity and the ability to strike fear into the most powerful countries.

I was awakened by a phone call. It was a young woman who was practically a child in 2014 and has been on the run since that very year. She cried as she explained that she really loves her new home—the city of Sloviansk, in eastern Ukraine—and never wants to leave it. She got my number from an acquaintance so as to ask about possible escape routes. I heard her tender, high-pitched voice—utterly incongruous with the sounds of gunfire and air defenses that, muffled by my tightly closed windows, have become the background to my everyday life.

DAY 34   *Tuesday, March 29*

Islands of Temporary Calm

When I began this diary, I didn't plan to pursue it for too long because I assumed the war would last only a few days. "It's really impossible," I thought, "that such a war won't come to an end at once. It's not doing anyone any good! The casualties are much greater than people think." The losses for Ukraine, Russia, and the entire world were already enormous on the very first day; every additional hour felt unreasonable and unnecessary.

The most important thing is to not turn around and reevaluate our previous experiences from our current vantage point. Every day at war is like a deadly disease that needs to be cured with urgency. When I wake up, I watch the news with hungry curiosity, expecting something to shift, expecting the values of the days before the war to be restored and validated at last. It can't be, I think, that the world simply watches as the residents of Mariupol are deported or slain in bomb shelters, as the people of Chernihiv are left to fend for themselves for days without food deliveries, as there is so much death, rape, plunder, and death again.

The tenderness of life is preserved on islands of temporary calm. And today I feel that is a rather daring, albeit inexplicable, thought. Even the soldiers I meet in the center of Kyiv seem to carry their former occupations within them—despite their weapons, despite having already been to the front. "What were you before the war?" I ask, and hear in reply: a lawyer, a mechanic. When I take their pictures, they ask me to delete the photographs. I always do. After the war, my files will contain almost no pictures of soldiers or ruins.

In the early evening, on Khreshchatyk Street, I met an elderly lady who was walking slowly because her small shopping bag was too heavy. We had been walking in the same direction for some time when she spoke to me. "Have you heard about the negotiations?" she asked. Despite the old lady's stark and hurried tone, she seemed much younger than her bent posture suggested. She was referring to the talks in Turkey between representatives of Russia and Ukraine. "How can we believe the Russians? Do you think that lives can be saved? After a hiatus they will surely attack us again." She uttered the last sentence with such disappointment, but also, I noticed, with a trace of hope in her voice. She belonged to those who still believe that this war is unthinkable and will promptly disappear, like a dream.

Today began with a report from Mykolaiv, in the south of Ukraine. The city hall had been shelled. A giant hole gaped in a house. A projectile tore something out of the middle of two connected buildings, as if a destructive force sought to pierce the heart of the city and put an end to urban life. Why does such an image spread so easily? It conveys something inhuman, a magnitude of destruction that reveals what's happening and on a more abstract level makes clear this alien pain. Only in the evening did it come to light that twelve people died in the rubble. The search for survivors continues.

Toward the end of the negotiations, I was euphoric for an instant.

I thought, this is a step in the right direction, some cities will be safer, including Kyiv. It means more lives will be saved.

As the negotiations went on, air raid sirens could be heard over and over again. On the street, I passed by groups of people who didn't dare leave the stores where they were shopping. They waited until the sirens ended.

As I write, I hear the sirens howling again.

The day before yesterday I met another elderly woman. She used to organize and direct something rather exotic for Kyiv: a fashion show. She was breathing heavily, walking behind me and talking as I kept turning to face her. Every day she walks five kilometers to a construction site, where she feeds animals whose owners have left the city. Several dogs and cats are hiding together at the site. They were left behind in Kyiv in panic and haste, and now they wait for these people to return, the ones they lived with whom they miss very much.

The lady explained how at the beginning of the war she saw a car loaded with suitcases and bags drive away, leaving a dog behind. A little boy cried and begged his mother to take the animal. But she sternly refused. The dog, which had a golden coat, ran beside the car for a long time, trying to catch up with it. Having witnessed this scene, the lady decided to provide food for the abandoned street pets of Kyiv.

When I returned home in the evening, I met a well-dressed woman carrying five dogs. She addressed them all with a jocular tone. She explained to me that these dogs, as well as the two cats waiting for her at home, were the only reason she had not left Kyiv. "It's not easy to travel with such a large party," she said. She looked happy.

DAY 35 *Wednesday, March 30*

In the Nerve Center of Catastrophe

The room I grew up in no longer corresponds to the life I lead—the life that is unfolding outside the window. As I look around, I realize it feels like a child's room that was abandoned a long time ago. And now I have to spend the night here again. The room tells a story of peace that I can't take seriously anymore as an "adult." On the shelf there are books in Russian, German, Ukrainian, and English. They seem to belong to another era. Since the start of the war, I have rarely opened a book, and when I do, I read no more than two or three pages.

The word "war" is even less comprehensible during wartime than in peacetime, when it's used quite differently. What is happening around me right now—the constant shelling and the warnings I hear—this is what "war" should mean. But this word seems meaningless, because in war reality breaks into parts, islands, pieces.

Next to the Kyiv apartment of an acquaintance of mine, buildings and houses are constantly damaged. In her own building, many window frames are empty: the glass has been shattered by waves of detonations. It is dangerous to visit her neighborhood. Not only are there damaged houses and cars, but mines and explosives have been strewn throughout small parks. In contrast, virtually nothing reaches this level of destruction in my neighborhood. I can think of only two or three routes that would lead to a dangerous zone if you were to walk for more than thirty minutes.

Another friend of mine from Kyiv hasn't been able to sleep at night since the war began. The strikes are too near, and she feels that her house could be damaged at any moment. She gets panic attacks and suffers heart pains, but she stays in the city, voluntarily distributing medicine and aid. Unlike her, I am often out in the street during the air raid sirens and always fall asleep at some point during the night.

The disjointedness of these experiences demonstrates that war and catastrophe have a local nervous system here in Kyiv. It is difficult for me to comprehend what is happening elsewhere, beyond the borders of the area I so rarely leave.

Lysychansk, a city in eastern Ukraine, borders Sievierodonetsk, which became the new administrative center of the whole Luhansk Oblast after the occupation of the region in 2014. Lysychansk remained an almost invisible little town, its existence mostly tied up with a coal industry in its death throes. I visited this town several times in the past few years to work on a photo series about the mines in the area. In my mind, I named this place "the City of the Fox" because you can hear lyssa, the Ukrainian word for "fox," very clearly in its name.

While traveling all over Lysychansk, the whole city seemed traumatized by the war that began in 2014. Many people told me stories of miraculous rescues, each with a variation on a singular inner voice that helped them escape death while they were under fire.

The war was terrible and it filled the city with fear. For the Lysychansk residents I met, any form of protest became unimaginable, even though the right to protest is an integral part of the political culture of Ukraine and has a long history among miners. I stayed in the only private hotel in this city, and there in my room I experienced my first serious feelings of fear and anxiety about Grad systems and rockets—despite the fact that I had already been to many cities in the Donbas.

It was a late evening in 2015. While on the phone with the receptionist, who told me how she had shielded her granddaughter with her own body for several hours during a bombardment, I approached the window of my room and heard a remote yet considerable roar. It was like a long rush of wind bearing metallic sounds. The roar seemed to be approaching us. The receptionist explained that this was the sound of missiles and that one couldn't simply hide when an attack happened. At that moment, I felt a profound, almost panicked urge to leave the city right away. Eventually I was able to calm down and convince myself to continue conducting my interviews.

Now I learn that the City of the Fox is under fire. Early in the morning, concrete apartment blocks were shelled, collapsing like houses of cards. I hear a confirmed update about a family: two small children were so badly injured that no one knows whether they can be saved. Legs may have to be amputated. The parents have been injured, but they will survive. The shelling endures as I write these words.

My Facebook timeline is silent about the bombardment of Lysychansk. Almost none of my friends have ever visited this city, which is a hermetically sealed world of miners and their everyday culture.

It was reported, after the recent negotiations with Russia in Turkey, that acts of war would be confined to the Donbas region. For me this means cities are being attacked that hardly anyone visits or knows much about, and that have already suffered from the Russian invasion for a long time.

DAY 37   *Friday, April 1*

A Changed City

It's getting harder and harder to write with regularity. The day of
my departure draws near, and this entry could be my last before I
leave Kyiv. I'll be leaving to arrange housing somewhere else for my
relatives, and to prepare this diary and my photographs for a group
exhibition.

After that I would like to return. I try not to scrutinize the purpose
of my departure over and over again. I've already changed my plans
twice and stayed in Kyiv, despite having bought tickets in advance.

When I walk through the city, I notice big changes. Every day a
new door opens—a new coffee shop, a new bakery or grocery store.
"New" means reopened in this case, but in my mind the city's former
life has been cut short, and so everything coming back into existence

starts from the beginning: the shop windows and opened doors face an absolutely different reality.

It's as if the whole city, with its streets, trams, curves, and worries, were shuttled to another location, while most of the pedestrians and passersby had gotten off at a previous station. And now that this great collective journey has taken place, it's especially difficult for me to leave and go somewhere else. Besides, the situation grows safer here with each passing day. At least I try to convince myself with this thought.

Yesterday evening I tried to choose a photograph from my files for a short radio report. I had planned to tell the story of a small volunteer center founded by three women that I had visited. But I couldn't find a single suitable picture. The three women—friends of a friend of mine—were packing baskets and plastic bags with food and hygiene products. Their names are Olga, Katia, and Yevgenia, and when they work, their graceful movements are so lightning fast that to capture their labor in a photograph is nearly impossible. Olga taught dance before the war. She founded a flamenco school in Kyiv.

The volunteer center operates out of a bomb shelter with walls painted a gaudy blue. I was moved by this jarring blue frame formed by the walls and doorways, so I tried to take a photograph as I was leaving. But right at that moment Olga spun around quickly, unintentionally but unavoidably blocking the shot, so the photo only captured her movement.

Several times Olga repeated the sentences: "Now there are volunteer centers like this one in every courtyard in Kyiv! The idea is that some of them will continue to operate after the war." Many people who remained in Kyiv would hardly have survived the war without such initiatives: mothers with small children who can't escape on their own; lonely seniors who hardly leave their homes but require medication. All this work is coordinated on Telegram channels, where requests for help are posted.

I myself joined the Telegram channels and know how difficult it can be to deliver medicine between the right and left banks of the Dnieper. Over the course of the war, the whole city has assumed a different shape; distances must constantly be measured anew and reinterpreted.

Fog, I noticed today, is the continuation of night: the darkness of day. Sunlight turns white and dense, prolonging the past. I felt as if I were standing with one foot stuck in yesterday.

On my way to the grocery store earlier, a car filled with bulletproof vests emerged from the fog. The vests were brought to the city for the Ukrainian army by another volunteer initiative. A woman who had fled the country organizes the manufacturing of these vests from her new residence. A group of her friends and acquaintances help to deliver them to Kyiv and the surrounding area.

My thoughts glide along these encounters and then fall into a chasm. A nineteen-year-old educational studies student named Anastasia tried to get to Chernihiv yesterday morning with food. Less than three hours to the north of Kyiv by bus, Chernihiv is one of the most beautiful cities in Ukraine, with cathedrals and monasteries that date back to the eleventh century. In many districts of the city now there is no electricity, no food, and no water. Anastasia had loaded a minibus with bread and medicine. It was obviously a civilian vehicle, but it was shot at on the way, along with other vehicles in the convoy. Anastasia died. The classmate of a good friend of mine also lost his life on the journey. Later I saw the photographs: her small, formerly white minibus was demolished in the middle of the road, blackened from fire and pierced with bullet holes.

Laughter Returns to Kyiv

A friend sent me a photo. In the photo small pieces of wave-shaped metal were embedded in her husband's hand. She included a note: "This is Grad." Grad is the name of one of Russia's most lethal missile-launching systems. I stared at the tender palm, its light pink tinge, and thought of the family of this friend, an artist I know rather well. Her name is Alevtina Kakhidze. Her mother died a few years ago on the border between the occupied region of the Donbas and the land still under Ukrainian control. Like many elderly people at that time, she had to undertake an exhausting and humiliating hours-long journey across the new border in order to collect her pension on Ukrainian soil. She didn't survive her last trip through the checkpoints. Alevtina had used her savings to buy a small apartment in Irpin for her mother so that she could convince her to leave the dangerous area. But her mother had hesitated because she loved her neighborhood and her garden, and felt bound to her house.

Alevtina's mother lived in the town of Zhdanovka. She didn't want to leave, on account of her garden. When she was still alive, she would tell her daughter stories about life under occupation, and her daughter would transform these words into drawings, quoting her mother's statements and descriptions. These were sketched opinions so to speak, and there was something immediate and childlike about them. Little was said officially and in the news about the town after 2014, once the Russian occupation began.

When I saw the hand in the photograph, I was troubled by the memory of another small town, Toretsk. I had visited this Ukrainian-controlled area of the Donbas several times while working on a photo series of a Roma family. I've only ever known this town in wartime—the last Ukrainian-controlled town at the border of the occupied territories. On the other side of the border is Horlivka, a somewhat larger and livelier city that used to be very closely connected with Toretsk before the war. Many people used to live in Toretsk and work in Horlivka.

Strange trees grow in Toretsk, even in the center of the city. Either they loom somewhat roughly pruned so that the long skinny branches tower over the tall, pollarded trunk; or the younger and thinner trees grow at a radical slant in contrast to the order of the streets, as if they're trying to overtake the city with the help of the earth's rotation.

In 2021 I discovered a flower shop not far from my hotel, which was the only hotel in Toretsk. The war was near and had already lasted seven years. You couldn't fail to hear the shelling like distant thunder that never fully abated. Many of the streets looked neglected. This bright shop on the other hand was well-maintained, displaying a wide selection of flowers and plants. The almost shocking domesticity of this flower shop would seem to suggest that the city's history wasn't bound up with the war.

The members of the Roma community of Toretsk lived close together, in private homes of all sizes in a residential part of town.

Whenever I visited them, I felt a ceremony in the air. Danger was always around the corner, yet we would listen to music and laugh together. The distant explosions of the ongoing battles dissipated in the laughter of my friends. I was so curious and even happy in Toretsk that the nearby violence of war was never a source of great fear for me.

Kristina Belous is one of the community leaders. She has a background in law and is the mother of five children, three of them adopted. To this day, she has remained in Toretsk with her entire family. We talked on the phone recently, and she told me that the village of Verkhnotoretske (Upper Toretsk) was no more than a ruin now. At the beginning of February, she started receiving panicked messages from the people of this village, asking for assistance, but there was nothing she could do. Since 2014, the village has belonged to the gray zone of the conflict: it is not controlled by either state.

The sixteen-year-old daughter of a friend of Kristina's lived in that village with her grandparents. A week ago, this girl set out and walked for days through forests, swamps, and fields in order to avoid the Russian checkpoints. She had no possessions with her, and she spent the nights alone in the cold darkness along the way, listening to the rumble of nonstop artillery fire. She reported that no house in her village had survived the shelling unscathed, nor does she know if anyone is still alive. The girl is so traumatized that she can hardly speak. All the telephone numbers of Verkhnotoretske are silent. You simply can't get in touch with the people of this village anymore.

I have never been to Upper Toretsk, and I can hardly imagine this settlement, along with the many towns and villages in eastern Ukraine with names that rarely appear in the news. Most of the people there speak a mix of Russian and Ukrainian. War crimes have taken place in the occupied territories since 2014, and now the towns on the Ukrainian side of the Donbas find themselves in danger again. Russia proclaims that they want to focus their attacks on this area. For their next crimes, the attackers choose the parts of the country that have already suffered so much in recent history.

In the evenings in Kyiv, you can hear laughter in the streets again.

But rockets are still fired at the city every day. As I edit this entry, the air raid warning has just begun to sound again.

It is much worse when it's not just rockets, but also artillery fire as the Russian army encroaches. In Bucha, a city northwest of Kyiv that has just been "liberated," the dead bodies of residents are lying in the streets. A mass grave with 280 bodies has just been discovered.

The whole world is speechless seeing the pictures from Bucha. Irpin and Bucha are places where many internally displaced persons from occupied Crimea and the Donbas bought and rented apartments. They could live there more cheaply and travel to Kyiv to work.

I ask all those who keep us in their thoughts—commit to memory the names of these unknown places in Ukraine. These are towns and villages where nobody could imagine a catastrophe of this magnitude. Very often these are the places where people go to start a new life with the hope of a new home. These places belong to us all.

All that has not yet been attacked must be saved. We must prevent any further destruction. This machine of annihilation threatens the whole world, and it is time to stop it. The sky over Ukraine must be closed. And if international politicians and heads of state are too cautious to do it, they can at least provide us with the means to do it ourselves.

Sunday, April 3

A City Drowns in Blood

A young man suffering from bipolar disorder, who lived all his life with his grandmother in Bucha, walked to the capital after his grandmother was shot by Russian soldiers in front of the entrance to her house. He completely lost his sense of time and doesn't remember how long he had walked on the road. For a few days he lived in Kyiv at the train station, where he met a policeman who took him to a volunteer center in the city where an acquaintance of mine works.

For days on end, a woman would not evacuate Irpin. She stopped responding to calls from her daughter, who was abroad at the time. Her friends tried in vain to persuade the woman to leave. Power in her apartment had already gone out and there was no water, but the woman stayed. Her neighbors refused to leave their high-rise as well. They tried to help the other remaining residents and care for the pets whose owners had left them behind. But the situation in the city became unbearable. In one of the last evacuation efforts, the neighbors were finally planning to leave and take the woman with them. But when they knocked on her apartment door there was no answer and the door was locked. Eventually she talked to the neighbors through the closed door, but she couldn't be persuaded. Fortunately, she survived the occupation of the city.

The father of a good friend of mine lives with his wife in Kharkiv. When the war began, they started a volunteer initiative to distribute medicine. My friend kept begging them to leave the city. But they stayed behind and helped many people. When the shelling and bombardment grew more intense, my friend's father suddenly disappeared. Several days passed before he was found. He'd had a paranoid episode in which he felt completely surrounded by enemies, death, and destruction. He couldn't trust his wife, his children, or his friends. In this delusional state of suspicion, he reached the Russian military posts, where he was wounded. Two or three bullets were removed from his body. He will survive.

Now I sometimes hear the casual assertion: "This person or that person was wounded." When it comes to health issues, gunshots and war wounds have nearly become a normalized form of harm in the collective imagination. Somewhere on the fringes of my childhood memories, I see children playing at being wounded soldiers. I myself liked to pretend that I was wounded. There always came a moment when I begged my friends in an unmistakable voice filled with suffering, "Leave me on the battlefield! I'm too much of a burden for you. Go on without me!"

Bucha is drowning in blood. When you hear of someone who has survived there, it is a miracle. The dictator claims that we are not simply related peoples, we are in fact "one people." But when you see what the Russian army is doing here—dead women who were raped on the side of the road in Bucha and Irpin, along with dead children—you understand immediately: This is a genocidal crime against all who have been dehumanized.

Today the streets of Kyiv were especially silent. The joy of return—quite faint, but still palpable only yesterday—was gone. The city mourned by being motionless and deserted of people. Sometimes I heard the whispered words, "Communal graves, mass graves..."

Kyiv—Warsaw—Berlin

The day passed at an accelerated pace. I left Kyiv, traveling for the first time since the war began. In the train car I heard passengers speaking Russian and Ukrainian. The direct route from Kyiv to Warsaw, created to help evacuate those seeking shelter, has existed for exactly one month to the day. The tickets were free, and people slept in small compartments—each containing three narrow beds—as well as the floor of the train's corridor.

Now you can also buy tickets for this train. Everyone has a little bed, and nobody has to sleep on the floor between bags and suitcases. Not too many people take the train in this direction now, and panic no longer reigns at the Kyiv station. The platforms were emptier than they had been a week ago.

My parents stayed behind in Kyiv. They wanted me to take the trip first and see if it was feasible for them, since my father still feels too weak to travel. I went with my cousin and her friend, who had been waiting for a chance to make the trip with company.

Somewhere along the way, I forced myself to take a picture of the landscape through the dusty train car window so that I wouldn't forget what I was going through at that very moment. But it was all for nothing. All these experiences and memories seem impossible to capture. The app on my phone that reports the latest air raid warnings in Kyiv chimed several times throughout the night. Like many other Ukrainians who have left the country, I didn't want to turn off the alerts.

I almost didn't get the chance to write because I wanted to spend time with the people in my compartment. I couldn't fall asleep either, busy listening to the faint, strange voices in the train car, each relating a story. These tales connected the travelers to the places they left behind—farther and farther behind with each passing minute—like a thread that stretches and stretches but never snaps.

"Why so much stuff—a giant suitcase and four big, hefty bags just for you?" one woman asked her neighbor, a younger woman named Dascha.

"Oh! I wanted to take so much with me, my whole apartment," Dascha replied. "Now I can barely lift this suitcase. Unfortunately, I left two of my favorite mugs in Kyiv! Instead I packed my straw hat with a red bow and my red velvet shoes that I can wear for work as well as the theater."

Yet Dascha, who spoke with a dreamy voice, had no more prospects for work, let alone plans to go to the theater anytime soon. In Russian and Ukrainian, as well as in German and English, the area Dascha left is described as the "theater of war." One rarely wears red velvet shoes to such a theater. Dascha lived on the outskirts of Kyiv, on the twentieth floor of an apartment building. During the early days of the war, she spent the night with her two cats in the bathtub because that was the only place she could fall asleep.

Then one of Dascha's friends called and invited her to share a room in a hotel for religious pilgrims. This hotel was part of Kyiv's Pechersk Lavra, a well-known cave monastery. The family of Dascha's friend lived in a picturesque area near Chernihiv. They had been living under Russian occupation for the past few weeks, along with two young relatives who had come to stay with them before the war. There was no water or electricity in their area, and food supplies were gradually running out. Every three or four days, they would go to their neighbor's house to charge their phones on a generator, and later call their daughter briefly before disappearing again.

Dascha called her friend's small hotel room at Lavra "a city unto itself." Life at the monastery followed a strict church schedule, with long morning services. No one thought it was necessary to go to the shelters during the air raids. The pilgrimage hotel and the monastery's huge residences were filled with people seeking shelter.

Another cave monastery—one of the most important Ukrainian Orthodox shrines which has also served as a residence for refugees since 2014—is located in the Donbas, in the small town of Sviatohirsk. Dascha had visited the site on a pilgrimage last October. She met families from Donetsk who had been living in the monastery since the beginning of the Donbas War—they were familiar with the area and refused to move to western or central Ukraine. Now the monastery in Sviatohirsk is once again overcrowded with a new influx of refugees.

Sviatohirsk is only thirty kilometers from Slavyansk, a town said to be the next target of Russian attacks. It's not clear how successful an evacuation would be—or whether one could be arranged at all. When Sviatohirsk's neighboring towns were being heavily shelled from 2014 to 2016, the faithful would travel to the monastery despite the danger. The daily environment in the monastery, shaped by the Orthodox routine, retained its peaceful qualities as if untouched by war. Three weeks ago, however, the monastery came under fire, with significant damage to the buildings where refugees were sheltering.

On the train, Dascha suddenly received some good news. Her friend's family, who had been out of touch for a full week, had apparently survived the occupation! In an emphatic voice, Dascha told the story of how a Russian soldier had once helped a woman in their family visit her sick friends in a distant town. She said the soldier accompanied her all the way there. The next moment, Dascha turned sad and despondent. Another friend had recently fled to Kyiv from Irpin, and Dascha suspects this friend may have been sexually assaulted. "She is a special woman, a talented photographer with a very soft voice. She's a gentle person," Dascha told me. "She can't talk about it. She's in such great shock that I hardly recognize her. Over these past few weeks, she has grown so much older. She hasn't said much about her escape but it's clear to me what she must have gone through."

Shortly after arriving in Warsaw, I walked through the city. The streets seemed sad and restless. I couldn't believe that there was no war here, and I saw in some of the faces of passersby the same worries expressed in the faces of Kyiv. Perhaps I was simply seeing the people of my own country, walking the streets just like me.

I saw a group of men in blue, official uniforms standing around chatting. I noticed with amazement that they carried no weapons. "So unprotected," I thought. "How could that be?" Then I realized once again the city's great fortune—that there is no war here in Warsaw.

The air was cool in Warsaw as it was in Kyiv. I thought I would probably spend the night in a part of the city without many pedestrians. I understand each empty stretch of street I see—emptiness is now familiar. In my mind I compare these streets with the streets in Kyiv, once full of people before the war but now remarkably empty.

Lately in Kyiv, everyday life seemed confined to a hiding place. Real life sheltered behind courtyard gates and the doors of volunteer centers, hospitals, bunkers, and apartments.

Gripped by waves of hope and despair for more than a month, many Kyiv residents wavered between grief for their wounded or deceased friends and an almost feverish preoccupation with the acute necessities of war. At the same time, many had no idea that in Bucha, Irpin, Vorzel, and Borodyanka, an unspeakable tragedy was unfolding.

We lived in a torn cocoon of grief, news constantly arriving through the cracks. I met refugees from Bucha and from Irpin, and they told me their stories, but the greater picture remained blurry and unimaginable until the past few days.

When I started this diary, I was convinced that I would only need to work on it for a few days. My faith in the impossibility of such a senseless war was strong.

Now I'm traveling onwards to Berlin, moving many kilometers farther from the ongoing violence. Looking out the window of the train at another country's sprawling landscape, I suddenly feel afraid for this new place as well.

The surroundings of Kyiv—a solemn, beautiful landscape where I once dreamed of having a small house—transform before our eyes into a giant memorial. Russia publishes manifestos in the state media to justify the mass murder of every one of us. The world considers what to do next. Some international experts play soothsayer and suggest that the war may last for years. In such ways, it seems to me, mass murder is indirectly legitimized. Every day of this war is one too many.

This diary cannot be completed, it can only be interrupted.

When you leave a war zone, you take a piece of it with you, as if by accident. This something remains glued to your life for a time, a souvenir you drag along and simply can't get rid of.

An employee at a hotel in Latvia calls a young woman in Amsterdam in the middle of the night. This young woman can sleep peacefully for the first time since February 24. She was able to organize the evacuation of her mother from Dnipro. Her mother has a weak heart and could hardly bear the sirens, the air raid alarms, and the thundering noises.

In a cozy hotel room in Riga that the daughter had anxiously rented for her mother, the air raid alarm blares from the mother's cell phone in the middle of the night. She never disabled the app that warns of an incoming strike. The mother gathers her most essential belongings, takes the elevator to the ground floor, travels a few steps to the reception desk, and demands to be escorted to the bomb shelter. If there really is no bomb shelter, she would agree to wait out the danger in the hotel basement. The hotel staff try, in vain, to convince her that in this peacetime city there is no imminent danger. The mother only calms down when her daughter is woken up at four in the morning by the hotel employee's call. Speaking to her daughter on the phone is the only thing that reassures the mother that the sky over Riga holds no threat to her life.

Another woman, whose husband was shot before her very eyes in Hostomel, outside of Kyiv, returns home to her family in western Ukraine. She didn't sustain a single injury. Saved! Her loved ones wait for her, for this woman who was an important figure in her town. For several years she ran a successful business in Hostomel that she had started herself. She arrives from liberated Hostomel practically empty-handed—no suitcase, no sack of personal belongings. Instead, she carries a small bag that holds half a piece of white bread, matches, a candle, and a small blanket. A strange survival kit assembled for war—the only possessions she had with her in the cellar where she hid with her husband when he was alive and then hid alone after his death. The kit replaces everything else she had owned, all the seemingly ordinary objects that in the course of evacuation had become so superfluous that they deserved to be left behind.

A few days ago we celebrated my mother's birthday in Berlin.

After my father's lung operation in Kyiv this past May, he spent his recovery in a special hospital for oncology patients. Wounded soldiers were stationed in most of the neighboring rooms.

The hospital is guarded around the clock by Ukrainian military and the Territorial Defense forces. The ground floor windows are barricaded with sandbags. To visit my father, I had to show my passport to the Territorial Defense and state my reason for entry. Despite the ongoing war, surveillance, and new security measures, the hospital felt warm and accessible each time I visited.

The soldiers at the front gate looked at me with a friendly expression; after my first visit they recognized me and let me through with less procedure. All the doctors in the hospital seemed to know everything. When I mentioned the name of the surgeon who performed my father's operation, a soldier remarked with almost childlike wonder: "This doctor is a god! Everybody knows what he can do."

The gate of the hospital quickly transformed into a place where I was greeted rather than inspected. The guards were always lending some small item to the sick, as well as to visitors. They helped to move heavy boxes into the hospital and, with their character and demeanor, they demonstrated that you could ask them for a favor any time.

Residents from all over the country would assemble in the hospital corridor by the surgeon's office—from the very ill and enfeebled to the courageous soldiers with their war wounds.

On our last visit, when my father's stitches from his operation were set to be removed, we sat in the waiting room next to a family sunken in thought. Both parents fixed their attention on their emaciated young daughter, who studied her surroundings with the wonder and disappointment of someone surprised by her own sickness.

Her mother approached me to discuss her daughter's medication, the effects of which she was having trouble tolerating. Their family came from Balakliya, a city in Kharkiv Oblast. On February 22, the parents decided to travel to Kyiv for five days with their gravely ill daughter for a consultation at the well-known clinic. They booked a hotel room and packed two suitcases with essentials.

The war broke out at just as their daughter's condition took a turn for the worse. She grew weaker and weaker. They didn't want to know about the war. They wanted to focus on their daughter's treatment.

Their own city, Balakliya, was under constant fire since the first day of the war, and then occupied since early March. Sometime later that month, the new administration told the city residents that empty apartments would be burglarized in order to requisition necessities. They used the phrase "burglarized" probably as a warning to those who chose to flee to Ukrainian-controlled areas that they would be dealt with harshly. While two generations of this family were in Kyiv, the grandparents moved into their children's apartment to protect it with their presence.

The family has now settled in Kyiv. The parents are constantly searching for small jobs and a permanent place to stay, as well for their daughter's medicine, which is in short supply. Their own city is inaccessible, growing farther and farther away. There are frequent power outages in Balakliya, so that when people try to call their family members, the phone lines are silent for days, sometimes weeks.

Husband and wife are so consumed by their daughter's illness that the war has become an oddity for them, a kind of intrusive disturbance that they assume will soon pass. They showed me photos of their beautiful, healthy daughter on the streets of Balakliya, and believed she would get well soon. Then they would return to their hometown and take walks together like before. And yet, so much damage has been done to the many buildings on the streets where they used to stroll and take family photographs. Some buildings have been entirely destroyed. The city changes every day under occupation without any announcement of these changes to the world. Everything happens as if behind a heavy curtain that conceals the stage during the play's intermission.

I call some acquaintances in Toretsk, a small city in Donetsk Oblast. The phone lines have been down for several days, just as in Balakliya. Toretsk is on the edge of the war zone, on the Ukrainian side of the conflict. The city's entire infrastructure has been destroyed, including its only school. Yesterday I saw pictures of a house there that had been destroyed by a missile. Five people were killed.

These people I called have been drinking water from wells around the neighborhood since March because the city water pipes have dried out. They use a generator and try to manage without electricity, often for a few days at time. However, such emergency measures are hardly sustainable.

A few days ago I spoke about evacuation plans with my friend, a human rights activist from the Roma community of Toretsk, but I couldn't make a strong case for my suggestion that she should leave. Of course, I realize she understands my objections better than I do, and if she does in fact choose to continue to stay, she must have her reasons.

In a bar in Berlin, a waitress from Ukraine tells me that Ukrainian doctors are returning to the hospitals in Mariupol. Her parents never left, hiding out in a dacha outside the city throughout the war. Despite the danger, this little one-story dacha was never hit. After everything her parents went through, the new administration of the occupied city forced a choice upon them: Either apply for a Russian passport or lose their apartment. And if they don't apply for passports are they supposed to leave the city? Nothing is clear in the occupied territories. Faced with this choice, the waitress's parents feel that, in fact, there really isn't any choice . They have nowhere else to go, so they decide to stay.

I visited a village on a number of occasions near Bucha called Moshchun, eighty-five percent of which was destroyed during the occupation of Kyiv Oblast. The family of a Ukrainian curator and art historian lives there. This family is now trying to renovate their house that was badly damaged but not completely ruined. During my visits, I would walk along the scorched streets. Behind the blackened remains of walls lining the roads, I often saw women tending their gardens.

They had stayed in the village, living in their own basements or with neighbors whose houses were still barely standing. Many of them chatted when they ran into each other on the street, and I listened to their conversations. I kept hearing, "Everything's good! We have our work, we've got a place to sleep, things are going just fine, at least through the summer. Winter—that's the one thing we're really worried about."

The inhabitants don't leave their demolished village; they take care of their gardens, which are far enough from their houses so as not to be shelled and burned. They live from day to day. In summer and even in late spring, people only stay indoors in a Ukrainian village to sleep. The day is usually spent outside, busy with gardening. So now life goes on almost as usual. And only now and again one remembers how cold the winter will be, and that the usual protections are lacking. It's a disturbing thought.

One does not want to accept the war.

Even I have to convince myself, persuade myself over and over again, that the war exists, that it endures, that I finish writing this entry in the midst of war. I talk to myself like a child, declare war on myself, and for a time that's enough. Hours pass, then days, until the wish to free myself from this fact overwhelms me.

I doubt reality and imagine I might wake up in a world where the war was never made real.

YEVGENIA BELORUSETS is a Ukrainian writer, artist, and photographer who lives in Kyiv and Berlin. She is the author of the collection of stories *Lucky Breaks*—"an essential document of our latest European war" (*The Washington Post*)—and the cycle of lectures *Modern Animal*. Her photographic work has been shown in the Ukrainian pavilion at the Venice Biennale in 2015 and 2022. She is a member of the Hudrada curatorial collective and cofounder of *Prostory*, a journal for literature, art, and politics.

GREG NISSAN is a poet and translator living in New York. He is the author of *The City Is Lush With / Obstructed Views* and the translator of *kochanie, today i bought bread* by Uljana Wolf. He is the recipient of Fulbright and NEA fellowships for translation.